Praise for *Faith Over Fear*

"In her four-plus years at ZipRecruiter, Mandy brought a contagious positivity and inspiration to everyone she interacted with. So it's no surprise that her first book, *Faith Over Fear*, is an absolute gem. It's filled with personal reflections and practical advice to help others harness the power of a growth mindset and chart a path to their own definition of success, one micro-goal at a time. Mandy provides many actionable insights to help anyone overcome their fears and make a lasting, positive impact on their life and the lives of those around them!"

—Ward Poulos, Cofounder of ZipRecruiter

"Mandy has been revered in our industry as an executive that creates success wherever she goes. And now she lets us in on her secret: that success is a state of mind. *Faith Over Fear* leaves us with lessons that we can all apply to our personal and professional journeys."

—Ryan Christoi, President of Recruitics

"I've known Mandy since before she joined ZipRecruiter in 2012. She was my account executive, and it was clear on our first meeting she had the 'right stuff.' Mandy is truly fearless, taking on one seemingly insurmountable task after another and crushing it. She is truly an inspiration to young women, showing her innate ability to jump over every barrier put in her way and excelling in—and sometimes out of—her lane to get the job done."

—Carl Braun, Job Board Pioneer, Podcaster Host/Producer, and Author of Twelve Books including *Recruit-Hire-Retain*

"*Faith Over Fear* by Mandy Schaniel is a must-read for those seeking a success mindset. Drawing from her experience as a business leader, Mandy shares personal stories and lays out keys to strengthen oneself for success, with a focus on faith, purpose, and leadership. Having worked with her since 2013, I appreciate her authentic writing and practical advice that make it easy for readers to follow in her footsteps."

—Kevin Gaither, Author of *It Happened on the Sales Floor: 100 Sensational Stories About Sales Leadership Screw-Ups and Big Wins* and Founder of InsideSalesExpert.com

"Mandy's personal story on learning to create and find success is a must-read roadmap for our own self-discovery and removing our limitations personally and professionally. As someone who has known Mandy for nearly fifteen years, her willingness to share her own story and vulnerability is honest and inspiring. She has blazed trails as a woman in a fast-growing startup in tech and continues to inspire others to take responsibility for all we do—good or bad—in order to achieve our goals and dreams. *Faith Over Fear* is a book for every business owner, professional, and person who has struggled with making the leap and removing those very individual constraints within our own selves that can hold us back. Everything is possible when you put your faith over fear."

—**Jessica Miller-Merrell, Author of *Tweet This! Twitter for Business* and Founder and CEO of Workology**

"Fear is real. It can and will consume you unless you know how to change it into faith. Life is short. When you know you have unfinished business or you're holding back from who you know you can be, when you know you can have the life you want and can contribute to your family, your community, and the world, you need to adopt Mandy's Faith Success Mindset.

I met Mandy while she was still in college and was fortunate to hire and mentor her through her early career. She has a drive and business acumen that is compassionate but results oriented. She is a true role model for all—but especially for women—navigating a male-dominated business world.

I've been fortunate to watch Mandy succeed, and I now have the privilege of having Mandy as a business advisor . . . and great friend."

—**Jonathan Duarte, Founder and CEO of GoHire**

FAITH OVER FEAR

FAITH OVER FEAR

HOW TO ADOPT A SUCCESS MINDSET

MANDY SCHANIEL

BROWN BOOKS
PUBLISHING GROUP

Faith Over Fear
How to Adopt a Success Mindset

Brown Books Publishing Group
Dallas, TX / New York, NY
www.BrownBooks.com
(972) 381-0009

A New Era in Publishing®

Publisher's Cataloging-In-Publication Data

Names: Schaniel, Mandy, author.
Title: Faith over fear : how to adopt a success mindset / Mandy Schaniel.
Description: Dallas, TX ; New York, NY : Brown Books Publishing Group, [2023]
    | Includes bibliographical references.
Identifiers: ISBN: 978-1-61254-623-0 (hardcover) | LCCN: 2023936794
Subjects: LCSH: Schaniel, Mandy. | Success Psychological aspect s. | Faith
    Psychological aspects. | Self confidence. | Self actualization (Psychology) |
    Leadership. | Fear. | LCGFT: Self help publications. | BISAC: SELF HELP
    / Motivational & Inspirational. | SELF HELP / Personal Growth / Success.
    | BUSINESS & ECONOM ICS / Leadership.
Classification: LCC: BF637.S8 S33 2023 | DDC: 158.1 dc23

ISBN 978-1-61254-623-0
LCCN 2023936794

Printed in the United States
10 9 8 7 6 5 4 3 2 1

For more information or to contact the author, please go to
www.MandySchaniel.com.

To my husband, for being my best friend, constant support,
and for always fortifying my confidence . . .
To my children, whom I pray will learn these lessons sooner than I did . . .
To my parents and family for always loving and believing in me . . .
To the many colleagues and mentors who lit a flame within me . . .
And to all the goal-getters out there who serve as inspiration.

CONTENTS

INTRODUCTION

"Action is a great restorer and builder of confidence. Inaction is not only the result, but the cause, of fear. Perhaps the action you take will be successful; perhaps different action or adjustments will have to follow. But any action is better than no action at all."

—Norman Vincent Peale[1]

Every day, millions of people wonder about success: how to reach it, what it means, what it looks like. Some of the most searched phrases related to success ask if success and happiness are linked, if success can be measured, if it can motivate a person, where it comes from, and what it means.

Based on my experience and observations, success is a mindset. Its definition (or destination) can vary from person to person or subject to subject (i.e., success at work, a successful relationship, personal success), but the common denominator between all types of success is the mindset it takes to achieve it. Unfortunately, as human beings, we seem to have a built-in, default roadblock that can steer us away from success without us even realizing it. In fact, we tend to justify the detour with logic and boost our confidence in the decision to avoid whatever lies beyond it. That detour is a four-letter "F" word that I absolutely despise. Fear.

The mountain of fear can appear at any time—the start of your journey, preventing you from even taking step one; in the midst of your journey, convincing you to choose another path; or even at the tail end, preventing you from reaching the finish line. One thing is for sure: becoming paralyzed by fear or letting it bring your journey to a halt certainly doesn't help you reach your destination any sooner.

Equal parts exciting and maddening to me is that despite how large and daunting the mountain of fear can seem to be, it can be completely demolished by my favorite five-letter "F" word. Faith.

When I tell people that I am a thirty-nine-year-old, retired startup executive, not only do I feel slightly awkward, but I also get an interesting range of reactions. Upon hearing the "R" word—retired—most people are taken aback, clearly thinking about how old they were or will be when they retire. This is what usually gets my humility and my wishing that I hadn't used the "R" word rolling. To be honest, at the start of my retirement while having ambitions to transition my consulting business to the broader field of leadership (business and personal), become an author, and bring all of the above to the speaker scene, I wasn't even sure if "retirement" was the right word to use when asked what I do.

Now, after months of figuring out how I define myself since retirement, I'll clarify that I am a retired, full-time stay-at-home mom who consults and coaches on the side and is finally fulfilling my dream to write a book and help as many people as possible using my experiences and the wisdom I've gained along the way. For me, retirement simply means working for myself on the passions I feel called to pursue. That said, most people are supportive and excited for me—and curious as to how I pulled off shirking the nine-to-five before turning forty! I've grown somewhat immune to the range of responses—"You got to that stage at this age?"—but I have always been aware of the emotions it can elicit in others. I've always wanted to share my "secrets" to success and help others experience the same, no matter their age or station in life. Because, in truth, there is no secret. The short answer is I had a whole lot of faith, made some great decisions, had an amazing support system, and have been incredibly blessed to see my faith and good decisions reward me handsomely. The magic ingredient to my successes and the successes of the people I use as examples in the following pages is faith.

My goal here is to use my experiences and those of others I find inspiring as a guide to help you find your way to success and fulfillment, whatever that may be for you, in hopes that you can also achieve incredible rewards for your good decisions and faith.

By faith, I don't mean to imply some mandatory belief in God—or any particular religion, for that matter. While God has been an ever-present source of grace, mercy, strength, and wisdom in my life, I have no desire to force my beliefs on others. I will share them with you, but please know that I am one of the most open people you'll ever meet. Let's just consider your reading this as us meeting, and it's quite nice to meet you. I personally enjoy learning about all different faiths, religions, and beliefs; I find so many similarities between the many different beliefs I've encountered and learned about, and I value everyone's journey—spiritual or not.

A comparative religions course I took at California Baptist University ended up being one of my favorite classes in college, and I encourage anyone with the time to take a similar course; it can only add to your existing belief system or help you find one. All that to say, think about my urging you to have faith as having faith primarily in yourself as well as looking at other sources out-side of yourself that you can have faith in and where you can grow in faith. Faith is a stronghold that will aid your success journey. Simply put, as you read the following pages, take what resonates with you and leave what doesn't. My hope is that the heart of this book will resonate with you and have an impact on your success journey.

With the benefit of hindsight, I can tell you that every major milestone that has gotten me to this point has been driven by that five-letter word, faith, which many people think has no place in a book about how to adjust your mindset to unleash success in all you do. My prayer for you is that this book will not only inspire you to challenge your default response to the bad that life throws your way, but also to drive impactful change for you and those around you. My goal is to offer the wisdom I've received from God (think spirit or the Universe, if you prefer) and experience. May these words bless you and all those in your sphere of influence.

Before we dig into setting the stage for your success path, I want to tackle the "woo woo," or rather the possibility that you may read some of my suggestions and think I'm a little "out there." Growing up Catholic, going to mass every Sunday and then Bible school or youth groups afterward until I was in high school, I can relate to thinking things like meditation, speaking of spirit or the Universe, or, shoot, even yoga as being pretty "out there."

I will never forget when Joan Osborne's song "One of Us" came out. I was eleven or twelve years old and acutely aware of the difference between my religious life and my secular life. I felt like I lived in two different worlds with two different friend groups, each interested in different topics and having different ideas about the world. This song was the first time I recall hearing someone speak of God so directly in secular music. I was ecstatic at the thought of those two worlds that I loved so very much becoming closer to one another! Imagine my excitement when I sat down to mass with my family, and "One of Us" began playing over the loudspeakers. I was over the moon! . . . Until the music stopped, and our deacon proceeded to admonish the nerve Osborne had to ask if the less-than-fabulous aspects of our human nature could be found in God.

I was so taken aback by this negative interpretation of the song I had been singing with *both* sets of friends and feeling like it bridged *both* of my worlds together, I couldn't wrap my head around what had just happened. That moment was when I started to question all that the Church had taught me was dangerous or too "out there" for a good Catholic girl to participate in or enjoy.

I began to seek freedom in a religion that allowed me to explore all facets of spirituality. I felt judged for loving that song, but I saw something bigger in that song being on the radio. I felt the same excitement the first time I heard a popular song with "Jesus" in the lyrics while my friends and I were enjoying a night of dancing at a local club. To me, it was moving to see everyone dancing and singing to a song about Jesus—spiritual and secular worlds colliding again in such a beautiful way before my very eyes. In truth, it opened my eyes to a dream to see more and more bridges being created between these two worlds I had grown up believing were so very separate. I don't condemn the Catholic Church for the admonishment of that song I saw so much good in, but it certainly stirred up a powerful belief in me that we, as humans, should encourage these bridges to be built and celebrated. To me, that belief was the secret to finally feeling free to be the whole me in every area of my life.

In my sophomore year of high school, I moved out of my dad's house to escape the toxicity of my then-stepmother and moved in with my mom. I have and always will be a daddy's girl, so that was not a decision I took lightly. The move meant starting a new high school a couple of months into the school year. I felt a bit lost: I'd left my friends. I'd left my varsity water polo team and now needed to fight for a spot on a much more competitive team. Despite the drama surrounding an investigation on whether the new school had recruited me, which was quashed by my former coach John Evans, I was allowed to try out and did make the varsity team. My new coach was also a Christian pastor; I became fast friends with one of his daughters, Jackie, and was soon invited to attend their church service. I found that freedom I had been searching for in Christianity, and the freedom has continued to expand as I've carefully explored things like meditation, affirmations, meditative yoga, and other forms of spirituality. I say all this in the hopes to open your eyes to the possibility that what you may think is "out there" might actually work for you and help you on your journey.

While you should be as cautious as you must to feel comfortable, keep your mind open. An open mind will serve you well. When I first stepped into leadership, I was perhaps too aware of my words when they crossed over from the secular to the spiritual. I treaded lightly in fear of offending anyone or leading someone to believe I was anything but open to the ways they found the strength or hope they needed in life. I've spent years reading books about leadership, success, and business, and what's eye-opening to me is the overwhelming theme that faith is a prerequisite to success.

Here I was thinking I was special (half-joking), but there it is—I'm not the first, and I certainly won't be the last to tell you how very important faith (in yourself and in something, anything, all the things bigger than yourself) is to your success. So as you continue to read and something feels a little too "out there" or "woo woo" to you, try to keep an open mind. It might be just the tool you need for your next big leap.

Either way, faith and a success mindset go hand in hand. Your mindset will determine your path and how close you come to reaching your goals, while faith—not fear—will get you to the right mindset. We'll dig into some practical ways to achieve both in these pages, so remember: keep your mind open to the possibility of your immense success and the new ways you might find it.

1

IDENTIFYING YOUR PURPOSE

As a child, I recall being acutely aware of the sentiment adults had about their jobs and, quite often, marriage and in-laws (it's always the Mother-In-Law, isn't it?!): nothing but dread, discontent, and endless complaints about horrible bosses (work), nagging or lazy spouses (marriage), and overbearing mothers-in-law (family). I remember from a young age being determined never to find myself stuck in a marriage or job that I didn't find fulfilling . . . and to have a great relationship with this seemingly impossible-to-love creature known as the Mother-In-Law (or MIL). I simply wanted to live a positive, happy life.

I credit my warp speed career growth, successful marriage of fifteen years (and counting!), and beautiful relationship with not only my mom and dad but also my MIL and all of my in-laws to my underlying commitment to finding the good in all things. To my mindset.

You might think I'm wearing rose-colored glasses. It's not that I overlook the negative or ignore it, but rather I *choose* to see the good—the growth—that comes with all of life's many circumstances. Don't think this choice is a suggestion to be a doormat; ask anyone who knows me—I stand up for myself and my community. But I always do my best to find the good in situations because, frankly,

I don't like feeling angry, frustrated, or stressed. I've found you have a greater impact on those you engage with when you assume the best of them, when you look beyond the surface level, and when you seek to understand what drives them. Let's face it, no relationship consists solely of positive interactions or situations. Instead of holding on to beliefs that someone with a particular role—say a boss or a spouse or an MIL—will always create issues, seek first to understand who they are and why they behave or communicate the way they do. You might be surprised to find that they aren't as "bad" as you once assumed they'd be. And I can almost guarantee your relationship and impact on them will benefit from this perspective.

To illustrate this point, let me take you back to a time when I hadn't quite honed the art of assuming the best. My husband and I had just moved away from our first home with our four-year-old daughter and two-year-old son. This was my first time living in Los Angeles, California, and my first time working in the office instead of from home since having my children. The move was exciting, as I was working on building out my first team and getting to experience my favorite startup in person every day. It was also stressful because I was getting used to the fact that a six-mile drive could take from forty-five minutes to an hour and found myself leaving the house before my children were awake and getting home after they'd gone to bed. It was a rough transition.

Just a few weeks into this new life, I found an opening to leave the office at a decent time and make sure I could spend some time with my children, do the bedtime routine, etc. So I took it and adjusted my hours so that I could get my job done and actually *seeing* my children could be a more regular thing. Soon after, I received a call from my boss, who worked remotely on the other side of the country. He had questions about my hours and made some comments that I heard as him insisting I be the first person in the office and the last one to leave.

As a mom, my heart was already breaking when my kids would melt down over not having seen me for a whole day, and while I didn't necessarily melt down, it was killing me as well. Instead of asking him to clarify, I pounced like a mama bear and made it clear in not-so-friendly words that there's two things you don't mess with me about: my money and my family. The conversation ended there, which was probably a good thing.

On my way out of the office, I ran into our CEO, who could probably see the steam coming out of my ears, and asked what was wrong. I explained the conversation, and he made it clear that, as a parent himself, he absolutely did not expect anyone to forego seeing their children for the sake of their job and encouraged me to speak with my boss again the next day.

I followed his advice, and after getting a surprising kudos for sticking up for my family, it became clear that my boss's intentions were to feel like he had eyes on the ground through me. What I hadn't realized, partially because he always presented himself as extremely confident and comfortable, was that he had insecurities about still being remote and saw me as a representation of himself in the office. Once I understood the reason behind his original questions about my hours and shared with him our CEO's stand on the importance of family and work-life balance, our relationship was pretty smooth sailing.

Do I regret going all mama bear on him? Perhaps I should . . . but frankly, I don't. It was a boundary-setting moment, one that ended in us better understanding one another and him respecting me more. The clarity I got from that encounter enabled me to assume the best moving forward and made me feel comfortable directly asking him what he meant, which saved me a lot of stress and potential hard feelings down the road.

The lesson here is that I'm not recommending you assume the best with no point of reference, but rather that you seek to understand whether that means setting boundaries, asking questions, or sharing how you perceived an interaction. Based on the response you receive, you can then tailor your best assumptions appropriately.

Everyone has the ability to achieve their dreams, to achieve the success they seek, and to achieve the life they wish to live—I strongly believe that. Most people get in their own way due to a lack of faith or success mindset, impatience, and/or a lack of understanding and clarity as to what they are trying to accomplish and the deeper purpose of it all. I believe there is a widely held misconception of what it means to live by faith. This does not mean not doing and simply waiting on God, the Universe, or someone in a position of authority to give you what you want. Sure, at times you will have to exercise patience (see chapter 6), but faith is a constant search—through thought, prayer, discussion, inward searching, and experience—of the right path or paths and actions that lead to achieving your dream.

ADOPT A STUDENT MINDSET

Know-it-alls, beware! Faith requires that you constantly assume the role of a student. There's no harm in owning your expertise and appreciating what you've already learned, but don't stop there. There is always something to learn in every situation, trial, or difficulty. It is certainly not easy, but once you adopt a student mindset, you'll see opportunity for growth and far more answers than when you weren't searching for them, thinking you already knew. It's uncomfortable, sure, but it's also incredibly powerful and game changing.

I've always been one to want to figure things out on my own. Quite literally, my first sentence ever was "I do it self!" While this natural desire to learn independently has led to a natural thirst for knowledge, a never-ending quest in my life, it can also prevent me from asking for help outside of myself and my ideas of where to gain the information or knowledge I need. I will never forget the first time I was asked to develop a hiring plan for my growing team at a fast-paced startup. This responsibility was given to me when, unbeknownst to me at the time, I was living through imposter syndrome. While proud of my rise to vice president of account management, I felt unprepared for some of the demands of my role and felt like I was surrounded by seasoned startup veterans who knew everything

I didn't. My first reaction was to panic and doubt my ability to do the job—yes, over a single task . . . This is what fear can do to you.

After my husband snapped me out of my fear and reminded me that I can do or figure out anything, I called on a colleague to ensure what I'd come up with was in line with what would be expected by the C-suite. It turns out, my logical brain (and research, lots of independent research) had nailed the structure of the plan. Had I not reached out for validation and help, I would have held on to my fears that everyone else with more experience at my level would have some tried-and-true template that I simply didn't know. That wasn't true, and turning to an outwardly student mindset saved me from further internal turmoil and doubt.

FIND CLARITY

"Stay away from what might have been, and look at what can be."
—MARSHA PETRIE SUE[1]

As I mentioned previously, lack of understanding and clarity on your goal or purpose can take you off your path to success. It can cause you to run in circles, feeling as though you are going nowhere. When you are a go-go-go type of person (raise your hand if you're with me), it can be incredibly difficult and feel almost painful to stop and take the time to identify what it is that you are after (go ahead and put your hand down now). A new friend of mine, Kimeral Anthony, a successful woman with expertise in risk management and insurance as well as a talented worship leader, shared this with me about the importance of clarity: "You have everything in you that you need to do whatever it is that you want, but you've got to get clear. What is it that you want?"

That's it right there. If you only scratch the surface on what it is you want to pursue, you're more likely to make the wrong turns and scratch your head, wondering how you ended up where you are. Again, if you're at that head-scratching moment now, it's all good.

There's no time like the present. Do the work now to identify clearly what it is that you truly want. Don't be afraid to pause and sit with your true goals and ambitions. In fact, it's quite important.

I've learned on my own spiritual journey how true it is that the spirit (or God, the Universe, however you prefer to refer to it) whispers. Quiet your mind and surroundings. Pause. Breathe. *Think.* Progress isn't always visible. We are thinkers, and we need to do thought work to gain clarity. This can come in the form of meditation, prayer, or even just "think time" that you block off on your calendar. Yes, do that—mark it on your calendar so you're more likely to do it consistently. Taking the time to think is imperative to your success.

What does that mean, and what does it involve? Self-reflection (go ahead and groan a little bit, I don't mind) is a great place to start. Instead of looking in a mirror and acknowledging your physical appearance, the practice of self-reflection is going inward and looking at yourself from the inside, recognizing the perfectly imperfect person that you are. Internally gaze at your behavior, your goals, and your personality. In the process, you will identify things you like and dislike. That's okay! The goal is to heighten your self-awareness and to become more honest with yourself. All of the above actually serve to increase your emotional intelligence, which will come in handy in every situation you encounter. The more time you spend inwardly thinking or self-reflecting, the more you'll be able to clarify your goal, find mini goals for self-improvement, and further arm yourself for the success you seek.

> TIP: Acknowledge that we, as humans, can never be perfect. Embrace the beauty of your imperfections, but never stop seeking to grow, learn, and improve in all ways possible. The goal isn't to be perfect, but to be the best version of you. Self-improvement is a powerful launching pad to identifying new goals and purpose in your life.

What is self-awareness? In short, being self-aware means having the ability to accurately recognize your emotions, thoughts, and values as well as knowing how they affect your behavior. This includes being aware of your strengths and limitations, your sense of confidence and optimism, and—something we'll touch on throughout these pages—a growth mindset.

Many psychologists and authors have written about the importance of self-awareness and call it by another name: Emotional Intelligence, or Emotional Quotient (EQ). Eric Jordan's book *Emotional Intelligence Mastery: A Practical Guide to Improving Your EQ* is a great read for those interested in better gauging their EQ and finding ways to further increase it.[2] Self-reflection—pausing and really evaluating your emotions, your triggers, how you react and respond to both the internal and external—is key to gaining an understanding of your EQ and identifying ways to increase it. Similar to your IQ, your EQ isn't set in stone.

Success means many different things to different people. If you don't take the time to stop and evaluate what it is that you seek, you're setting yourself up for a series of frustrations and a feeling like you've wasted quite a bit of time. If this is hitting home for you, all is not lost. Perhaps you've been on a circular journey thus far and have poured months or years into a pursuit that, after deep thought, you realize is no longer your purpose or getting you toward your goal. Acknowledge how you feel about that and then look for the learnings in that journey, however pointless you may initially feel it has been. Nothing is ever wasted if you invest the time to learn. There is no such thing as failure so long as you learn from your mistakes and experiences. It's all part of the journey, my friend.

You also shouldn't feel compelled to remain committed to a pursuit that no longer gives you purpose or fulfillment. It's quite alright to change paths. For me, career growth came early and quickly. My climb up the career ladder led me to constantly pursuing the next rung; it was almost addictive. I made a few job changes in search of greater fulfillment, only to realize that what I truly valued was balance in my life.

The constant pursuit of the next rung certainly didn't make it easy to balance my home life with my work life. I reflected on the fact that my pursuit kept pulling time away from my husband and children. As a child, I never really set my sights on a particular career. In fact, my clearest future goal was to be a wife and a mom. The realization that my addiction to the next rung was pulling me away from my greatest missions in life led me, in small steps, to shift course: first by starting my own consulting business, then by moving my business away from purely business and into a more well-rounded practice of consulting on leadership (both personal and professional). And now, you're reading the final step: taking all I've learned and sharing it with as many people as possible while still working for myself and structuring my life in a way that allows me to prioritize my greatest blessing—my family.

Use the lessons you've gained from each path you've taken, and you'll be better prepared for the next one. Commitment and loyalty are important character traits that should be developed, but commitment for the sake of commitment when the situation is toxic or unhealthy despite every effort to improve it is not a good thing; it's more like torture. Again, this is why it's important to slow down to gain understanding and perspective—clarity—on the path you're on. You need to decide whether more effort needs to be poured into improving the "road conditions," or if it's time to realize the road is treacherous and can no longer be traveled safely. Show some commitment and loyalty to your own well-being by stopping to evaluate this. Be honest with yourself about the work that needs to be done and whether the work will make a difference.

Here are some questions you should never stop asking about the path you're on:

◊ What can I learn from this experience?
◊ What could I have done differently?
◊ What was the purpose of this experience?
◊ How can I apply these learnings to my next experience?

MINDSET

Another key component to setting yourself up for success is your mindset. While faith and positive mental attitude are often used interchangeably, they are different but *powerfully* compatible. One could argue that, by nature, true faith requires a positive mental attitude. And while I don't disagree with that, I know from personal experience what it's like to feel like you have faith but suffer from a negative subconscious.

In my case, focusing on improving my mindset from negative to positive made it much easier to rest on faith and find my path and purpose. I'll explain this further, but know that your path may consist of big leaps of faith, a million little stepping stones, uphill treks, scary cliffs, perhaps some seemingly dead ends . . . quite likely all of the above amid a winding road. Don't let obstacles or even those apparent dead-ends kill your positive spirit or hinder your faith. They are part of the journey and wonderful tools to test and refine you. Keep the faith, search for the opportunity to grow—you'll be better for it and much further along than if you'd stopped to rock gently in a corner submitting to what you think means failure.

For the record, failure is a wonderful tool on the path to success. Failure presents the opportunity to identify what needs to be learned in order to try, try again, and eventually succeed. Disappointments can also steer you off course if you haven't adopted an Act As If mindset.

Imagine you're Edwin C. Barnes, a man who had a deep desire to become business partners with Thomas Edison himself. Barnes spent years transforming that dream into a strongly held desire that he had conviction in seeing through. When he arrived at Edison's doorstep, he was offered a menial job—not a partnership.

How would you react in that situation? Would you give up and walk away?

Or, like Barnes, would you continue to stay committed to your conviction and work for five years doing menial work as though you were already business partners with someone you admired and find the most opportune time to make a case for that partnership to come to fruition?[3]

Giving up is the easy way out. Sticking to your dream, your desire, your convictions in the light of obstacles and disappointments will help you to gain momentum. To clarify, I'm not suggesting that everyone has to start at the bottom and wait years and years to achieve their initial goal; that said, there will be times when you have to adjust your expectations and put in time to get to the level you want to be. By all means, openly discuss reasonable timelines and evaluate whether you are willing to put in that amount of time, and certainly ask around to confirm whether the timeline you are given for growth is actually reasonable.

In my career as both an employee and a leader, I've found the Act As If attitude to be a tremendous asset. Every promotion I received led to another goal and another opportunity to prove myself by acting as if I was already in the next role I sought—not in ego, not from a holier-than-thou place either, but by acting the part in my work ethic, raising my expectations of myself, increasing my confidence, and always seeking to find what else I needed to learn to be successful in the new role I was embodying. Across all the people I've managed, I've given the advice to Act As If, especially to those with high-growth ambition. Each and every time, when we were able to harness that Barnes-level desire and commitment to making the dream a reality, we were successful. This isn't a quick fix, and it may well take years as it did for Barnes, but stay the course, focus on your mindset, and ensure it's leading you down the path to success.

So often, we fear the dream itself and play a defensive angle with backup plans and safety nets. However you approach your goal and the possible threat of disappointment, defeat, or failure, consider what that mindset is telling your subconscious: if your focus becomes all about how you'll bob and weave if it doesn't work out, do you think that's strengthening or weakening your resolve, your commitment, to seeing the dream realized? I am a planner, so in order for me to fully focus on and dedicate myself to achieving a goal, I do need to consider all scenarios and potential outcomes. Once I've wrapped my brain around all of that, I move it aside and stare down the barrel at my end goal.

For a little more than a decade, I have been the primary bread-winner in our family, with my husband serving as Household CEO. I fully understand the need to ensure all mouths will continue to be fed regardless of what dream or goal I am chasing, but what I've learned time and time again is that I succeed more easily and in bigger ways when I take a leap and feel that risk sensation so many of us work hard to steer clear of. Giving yourself too many outs only increases the likelihood of giving up when the going gets tough. And if you're reading this, I think I can confidently say that's not what you're about.

The truth is that my faith and positive mindset have gotten me, quite literally, everywhere I've wanted to go—even when I didn't re-alize it. One of the most impactful and beautiful lessons I've learned is that when faith confronts fear, the impossible happens.

To help you understand more about me and my story, I'm going to take you back to some pivotal moments in my life in hopes that they resonate with— perhaps inspire—you to adopt a deeper faith in yourself, your god, the Universe, and the importance of remaining positive.

As I mentioned, I knew as a child that I simply wanted to be hap-py. I committed to finding the good in each experience and person I encountered. I learned to look for the Why in the behavior of others and see them for their potential. Chances are that doing so will help them see it as well and leave a positive mark on their life. I'd call that a gratifying win.

I learned early on that I'm the type of person who is most suc-cessful when I have a lot on my plate; otherwise, I'm slightly prone to procrastination and boredom. During college, I found it easier to focus and achieve solid grades once I began working full-time and taking a full class load. Sure, I could have complained about how little time I had for hanging out with friends, but I found it nearly intoxicating to have the opportunity to learn so much in such a short period of time. It fueled my desire to grow and grow and grow. It made me happy.

> *TIP:* **Take the time to learn what makes you tick. What gets you up in the morning (aside from one or seven alarm clocks)? What gets you excited to work hard? What causes you to slow to a halt? Can you find ways to incorporate more of those exciting elements to propel you forward on your path that much further? Give it some thought. You might be surprised by what you learn about yourself.**

Have you ever heard the story of George Dantzig? You may remember the movie *Good Will Hunting*. Well, he was the real Will Hunting, and he famously solved two open problems in statistical theory that he had mistaken for homework because he arrived late to a lecture by Jerzy Neyman.[4] Think about that for a moment. Two famously unsolved statistical problems (theorems, actually) solved because someone didn't have the preconceived notion that they were impossible to solve.

In my experience, some of the fastest ways to achieve massive growth are to prevent yourself from doubting your ability to succeed and to avoid fearing failure. If you don't let yourself think something is impossible and you're sure to fail at it, you might just solve what others deem unsolvable. This is why it's so important to activate your thirst for knowledge in whatever subjects you find interesting. You will have to make choices about how you allocate your time to achieve the learning you want and need, but you'll grow in ways you might not expect, find ways to connect the dots between what you've learned and problems you need to solve, and wind up that much closer to your goal.

> *TIP*: Be a sponge. Learn to love opening your mind (and heart) to learning new things and challenging preconceived notions and beliefs. This can be difficult, but think about a sponge that doesn't take on water. It quickly becomes dry and crusty. A sponge that absorbs water is full, plush, and pliable. You choose: dry and crusty, or plush and pliable? (And yes, I'm cringing at this metaphor . . . but it works.)

Soon after graduating college, I found myself at a crossroads. With my degree in communications (emphasis on print journalism—hey, I'm finally using it!), I faced two opportunities that I knew would take me down drastically different paths and alter my future: on one side was a junior copywriting position at a local newspaper that paid a bit less than what I was making as a hybrid administration assistant/ account manager/tech support rep (startup much?). On the other side, there was an opportunity to make significantly more money and further expand my growing industry knowledge and network as a full-time sales rep—something I never thought I'd be.

I took the sales job after reviewing the pros and cons of both opportunities. Why? I was honest with myself about my goals at the time and was able to convince myself that sales does, in fact, require creativity, something I worried I might mourn when choosing sales over writing. I quite literally sold myself on taking the sales job. I took a somewhat unconventional approach to sales: I didn't obsess over my quota, I didn't push a close with a prospect who didn't have a need, and I was honest about what to expect from the service. I declined taking money from any client who wasn't a good fit; it just wasn't the right thing to do. Shocking to me, I was quite successful.

Better yet, I felt a sense of fulfillment in helping solve problems for my clients. Working in digital advertising for recruitment, it certainly didn't hurt knowing all my work meant helping employers fill open positions, thus helping people find jobs. I soaked up industry knowledge as fast as I possibly could, my network grew exponentially, and just as I had gained some self-confidence, I realized I felt I'd hit a ceiling on my growth. I'd outgrown that company, but I was equally attached to and grateful for the opportunity it had provided me.

> *TIP:* It's important to recognize when you're using a sense of loyalty against your future growth. Loyalty is a wonderful trait, but in situations where you start to see the next stepping stone, don't allow yourself to use loyalty as an anchor, or you'll never move to the next stone.

While I felt I had learned as much as I thought was possible in that role and at that company, I wasn't happy and had fallen into the cycle of dread, dissatisfaction, and (pet peeve alert) constant complaining about my job, but I didn't know how or if I could move on. I went from fork in the road to high point (success in the new role and fulfillment) to low point ("Oh, crap, I don't like this anymore. I've outgrown where I am.") in the span of about five years.

> *TIP:* Learn to identify the stepping stones. Regardless of the span of time, the important thing to remember when you go on this kind of roller coaster—in work, life, relationships—is to stop and identify where there are opportunities to learn, whether growth and change on your part will remedy the situation, or whether it's time to recognize the current situation as a stepping stone and begin looking for the next step (or leap, in some cases). Take the time to understand where and why you are where you are and strategize what is the next right move.

I didn't know how to get out of that rut, a rut I'm sure you're familiar with or dealing with right now. I lacked the confidence I needed to find a better fit, and even doubted whether I could hack it at another sales job or make what I was making despite knowing I was worth what I was making and more.

That all changed when I got a phone call from my dad in the wee hours of the morning, letting me know that my estranged half-brother had been in a horrible accident and might not make it. I may have been estranged from my brother, but I, of course, still cared and have always had a close relationship with my dad (Daddy's girl, remember?), so there was no way I was going to let him sit alone at the hospital wondering whether one of his children was going to live. After filling my husband in on the situation, I left for the hospital and what would wind up being a two-week roller coaster ride consisting of driving back and forth to the hospital and home, eyeing my dad carefully to make sure he was okay, having to come face-to-face with estranged family members I never intended to see or speak to again, and praying. Like face-in-Bible, nonstop praying.

My brother made a miraculous recovery from a traumatic brain injury, one that I am absolutely certain we prayed into existence. (When I say "we," I must give at least 90 percent of the credit to my nana who carries a direct line to God via her rosary beads.) God worked in me like never before. In all my Bible verse searching for the right words, greater faith, and some peace during his coma, surgeries, and recovery, an attitude adjustment came my way, freeing me from Complainers Syndrome. Life-or-death situations have a funny way of making you think long and hard about how you want to live life and who you want to be. I'd always known I didn't want to be Complainer of the Year. Quite the contrary, I've wanted to be a motivational speaker since I was seventeen. I could no longer justify my attitude about my work situation or let my loyalty be my anchor. Regardless of where I wanted to point my finger, I knew I could only control my attitude and my response to everything I no longer desired in my situation.

I highly recommend the Bible as a source of wisdom, answers to your biggest questions, and a guide on how to find the blessing in every situation. Don't get me wrong, there are many situations in life where there is distance between a bad situation and finding the good, but there's one thing for certain: *you* are in control of how you respond to the situation and whether you seek the good or hold on to the bad. I recommend the former.

> **TIP:** Put your trials to use by finding the good in them. Every bad thing thrown your way is an opportunity. You can hold onto and collect the bad, or you can give every bad situation a good squeeze, even if all you're able to extract is a single good seed such as, "Well, now I know how I don't want to be treated." Or "Hey, now I know how to deal with that kind of person." Or even "Welp, I'll never do that again." If you spend your time and energy finding whatever good you can get, you'll soon notice you are surrounded by good and better able to find good in both the good and bad. You'll be so focused on the good that you'll have a brighter outlook AND you'll attract more good into your life.

So I decided to put my life verse and sarcasm to good use. My life verse is Jeremiah 29:11.

> *"For I know the plans I have for you," declares the Lord, "plans to prosper you and not to harm you, plans to give you a hope and a future."*
> —JEREMIAH 29:11 (NEW INTERNATIONAL VERSION)[5]

That verse found me during the September 11 attack on the Twin Towers, at a time when my father was still a police sergeant, and I found myself full of fear that something may happen to him—despite being on the other side of the country from the attacks. I will never forget the feeling of togetherness that was widely felt in America in the days after one of the most horrific events we as a country have experienced. That experience reinforced my faith that any and all situations in life could ultimately be used for a good purpose. In the moment, devastation and tragedy are impossibly hard to understand and it can take time to work through all of the emotions that come with it. Time and again, I have seen good ultimately come out of those situations in some way, shape, or form . . . if and when you seek it.

As we neared the success point for my brother's healing, it was becoming abundantly clear that the scare with my brother was intended to wake me up. Not just for that, of course, but that was one of the goods that I was blessed to experience as a result. Nothing good was coming from my cycle of frustration and complaining. It certainly didn't feel good. I decided—somewhat as a challenge to God if I'm being honest—to catch myself in each frustrating situation and flip it. Instead of allowing myself to get into that negative complaint cycle, I'd acknowledge the situation for what it was and reaffirm my faith that there would be a blessing on the other side of the situation.

Figure 1.1. Two cycles repeating various types of complaining

Not only did this build my confidence in making the leap to the next stone on my journey, but it also allowed me to untether my loyalty anchor. There were many times in which the situation would continue or cause me more frustration (mostly on my part for holding on to that anchor with a death grip), so I'd sarcastically exclaim, "Oh wow!

It's going to be an even bigger blessing. I am so thankful for this!" Not for nothing; it's pretty therapeutic to express your dissatisfaction in this way. (I mean, if you get joy out of being sarcastic . . . which I do.)

> **TIP:** Use your personality to your advantage and learn how to reprogram your responses to avoid a negative cycle. By all means, feel free to try my sarcasm flip method if it suits you.

What happened next surprised me. It did not take long for my mental trick to reboot my default reaction to those frustrating/stressful/negative moments. Not only did this mindset hack make it easier to tolerate the situation I was in, but it also improved my relationships and soon brought . . . you guessed it, some pretty tremendous blessings my way.

TAKE THE LEAP

After nearly five years in that sales-turned-customer-success-and-business-development job, and just five months after my brother's traumatic brain injury that led to my mindset hack, twenty-eight-year-old me received a job offer that would quite literally change my life. Here I was, doubting whether I could be successful elsewhere, and in comes a startup founder that I highly respected who had kicked off recruitment by informing me that I was one of the best and worth recruiting—something I always sought but truly didn't believe about myself at the time. His confidence in me and no-nonsense urging that I own my expertise left a lasting impression on me and set me on a path to want to be that for as many people as I could. To empower and push them on to the wild ride of career success like he did for me. That man was none other than CEO and cofounder of ZipRecruiter, Ian Siegel.

TIP: Find what makes you tick. For me, being a helping hand, mentoring, and leading others gives me an incredible sense of fulfillment. The impact Ian's confidence and guidance had on me was so significant, it made me want to follow suit. Once I realized those aspects of my role inspired me the most, my path became clearer. I assure you that taking the time to learn what inspires and fulfills you will help you to see further down the road to identify the next stepping stone, obstacle, or chasm to conquer.

Working at ZipRecruiter was the most amazing experience. There's really no other way to describe it. The culture was everything I'd ever wanted, everything I'd imagined working at Google in the early days was like; we didn't have a slide in the front office, but we did have a kitchen full of free snacks, games, and an energy that just filled me with so much excitement and inspiration . . . almost like your-life-turning-into-a-musical kind of awesome. I was surrounded by people so intelligent that I used to joke that you instantly gained IQ points just by walking into the office. Even more amazing to me then was that they all seemed to respect my opinions and love my ideas—okay, maybe not *all* of them—and empowered me to continue sharing them.

I was used to a scrappier kind of startup environment. You know the one: you wear so many different hats that you're not sure what your job title should be; you can easily feel overworked, undervalued, and like you don't have the level of support to accomplish what you know you're capable of. So you definitely don't think you're worthy of being proactively recruited by what you knew from day one was going to be the "Google" of your industry. And so out of confusion, lack of confidence, and guilt, you almost turned down the most pivotal change in your life.

Yeah, that kind.

After experiencing that game-changing moment—being recruited and complimented by someone I so deeply respected (and still do)—and realizing that I *could* have everything I ever wanted in a job, I decided I wanted in on more of those moments and to be the one giving them to others. I figured other leaders did too. Despite my previous experiences with some leaders who left something to be desired, I always chose to watch and see what I could learn, chucking out the not-so-great traits from my list of leadership qualities I aspired to master.

My personal career journey led me to wear rose-colored glasses about business leadership, despite not magically being surrounded by the most inspiring leaders 100 percent of the time. I want you to understand why. I could give you a long, drawn-out list of my career history ranging from being a cashier to lifeguarding and swim instruction (side note: teaching Tiny Tots is one of my favorite high-school-job experiences), to file clerk, to sales assistant, and so on. You might not care about those experiences, but what you may want to know is that over the span of seventeen years, I managed to grow from a temporary File Clerk to an Executive Vice President of Client Success and founder and CEO of Schaniel Consulting Inc.

The first big jump came about six years into my professional career, when the opportunity to take on the role of director of business development came to me due to the departure of my boss. The pace of my career growth accelerated at that point, bringing me to my first vice president title (VP of account management and optimization) within a year of reaching director—I call that my ZipRecruiter jump and my first real role with consistent management responsibilities. I stayed at the VP level for four-and-a-half years until I felt stalled in my growth and was recruited into a senior vice president of customer success role. While the environment I found myself in wasn't a fit for me long-term, I realized just how badly I'd needed to confirm for myself that I could hack it at another non-startup at a VP level. From there, I left to figure out my next move, which led to becoming founder and CEO of my own consulting business and moonlighting to help an early-stage startup get off the ground.

That startup, while still around today with great promise of being successful, never really took off during the two years I was focused on it. I was feeling the effects of burnout after my four-and-a-half years at the non-stop, rocket ship ride at ZipRecruiter combined with moving into a higher level role. This was after moving my family from Arizona to California with less than three weeks between the job transition. On top of that, my dad's cancer that had been in remission for a few years had returned. Immediately after taking my step back to only advise that startup and contemplate how to expand my own consulting business, I received a call from an old colleague . . . with a consulting gig.

That consulting gig was always intended to lead into a full-time position, which I resisted until my youngest son was in preschool. With all three of my kids in school for some portion of the day, I agreed to join TruckersReport.com full-time as executive vice president of client success with the understanding that once ZipRecruiter went public via an initial public offering (IPO), I would likely be in a position to retire from full-time work.

I share all of this with you not to brag, but to prove a point: faith and self-leadership are the two most important aspects to achieving success. I have certainly been blessed to work with some pretty amazing leaders throughout my career, but I've also worked with some not-so-great leaders. No, I won't name names, and I'm happy to report many of them have grown and become better leaders over the years.

I've experienced working with leaders whose distrust of me or any employee caused me such severe stress that it actually affected my health, a few who couldn't care less about my personal growth, the credit thieves, and even some incredibly old-school leaders who thought they were doing me a favor by suggesting I randomly fire members of my newly inherited team upon joining the company, in order to "earn respect" . . . because, you know, who would respect the youngest woman executive that company had ever hired?!

For the record, I voiced my beliefs on how ridiculous that suggestion was and did not comply. Thankfully, this didn't create any issues for me, as I politely reminded him that this is the type of thing they recruited me for, and that ultimately he could judge me on the performance of my team—as my compensation plan depended on it.

Throughout each of these experiences, I chose to learn what I could and make a mental list of all the ways I wouldn't lead my current or future employees. That's not to say I always responded gracefully to those less-than-stellar moments, but when push came to shove, my faith mindset enabled me to see how I could grow . . . sometimes despite the leaders I was stuck under.

As I worked to become the kind of leader who could have the sort of impact on my teams as Ian Siegel's faith and confidence in me had, I sought advice and examples from books, articles, and, of course, the leaders and organizations I encountered. (Have no fear, I'll make several book recommendations throughout these pages. Here's one of my favorites: *Creating Magic: Ten Common Sense Leadership Strategies from a Life at Disney* by Lee Cockerell, a book I recommend to every new leader, current leader, and anyone with leadership ambitions.[6])

So why do I share this with you? To explain that the phase of success I call identifying your purpose can be one that takes quite some time. For much of the phase, you may feel confused and often frustrated. Remember when we talked about lack of clarity and understanding earlier? That sums up pretty well the majority of this phase, however long it will last.

One thing's for sure, moving on to the next phase, discovering the why, will undoubtedly be brought on by a significant moment or realization. It could be an experience that elicits a strong reaction from the inner depths of the self, or a lightbulb moment that suddenly awakens you to a strength you never realized you had.

Now that you have taken the time to clarify your goal, adopt a student mindset, and reflect on your faith, you are equipped to discover your why and create stepping-stone goals on your path to success.

2

DISCOVERING THE WHY

The realization that what I had dreamed all my life about work could be true, and I could have a hand in making that happen for others as well, was my aha moment. Often, moving on to the phase of discovery is preceded by a moment like this: one that opens your eyes to a passion, a strength, some type of longing. It might be an event that evokes a response like, "I'll never let that happen to someone else," or, "I'm going to show everyone that not all [*insert something you identify with or choose to become*] are like that." But rest assured, it is these moments that propel us on to the most fulfilling of success paths.

We touched on finding clarity in your goals, but now we want to discern the Whys behind those goals. This phase of your journey is easy to rush past. Let's say your primary goal is career oriented. It may feel silly to take time to delve into the Why when something like that seems so cut-and-dry. Often, the simplest seeming goals are surface level. Example: your goal is to make $100,000 a year. That sounds simple enough; but if you fail to identify the Why(s), when you face challenges—which generally elicit some type of emotion related to fear—you are more likely to give in to the fear and abandon your goal. With one or more clear Whys, your faith response is more likely to kick in and help you use that fear productively instead of letting it come between you and your goals.

DIG DEEPER

It is key to develop one or more Whys that are deeper than a seemingly surface-level goal. For example, your Whys for making $100,000 a year might be to provide a better life for your family or to buy a home instead of renting an apartment. Unpacking the reasons behind your goal allows you to detail steps, micro-goals, on the way to what is often a big, hairy, audacious, and daunting goal. We'll get to those goals later.

First, ask yourself these questions:

◊ **Why do I want to achieve this goal?** Identify two to three reasons why this goal is important to you.

◊ **What does this accomplishment mean to me?** Think long and hard about how you'll feel when you complete the goal. Will it affect how you feel about yourself? Will it validate your confidence in taking on another bigger goal you've wanted to achieve but haven't had the courage to go after yet? Do you have something to prove to yourself or others? Dig into every aspect of meaning behind this goal.

◊ **Who else will my success impact and how?** Aside from what you will get out of this achievement, who else will benefit from your success? Your children, your spouse, your employees, the public?

◊ **What will this achievement allow me to do next?** Without getting distracted and wanting to jump to your next goal, think about the possibilities that will open as a result of this achievement. See the road you are carving out for yourself.

By spending some time answering those questions, you'll unearth the reasons at the heart of your desire to achieve whatever goal you're after. Your answers to these questions will become additional tools to keep you going when the path becomes difficult. They're like roots, firmly planting your goal seed in fertile soil—more grounded, more stable, more difficult to move. Too often, we simplify our goals, our reasons, and the results we expect to see from achieving said goals. Shrinking the impact of success makes it easier to walk away when the going gets tough, but painting a picture of how far and wide the impact of our success can be makes it more real and much more difficult to give up on.

The process of writing this book has continually reinforced the necessity for a deeper Why for me. Just wanting to write a book would never have been enough to actually get it done. Not with the scheduling demands of having three children, beginning a new consulting contract, and learning how to be retired at the same time. In the moments when doubt or frustration would start to creep into my mind, God always found a way to bring up a conversation with a friend, family member, or client on the exact lines of what I'd been writing at the time.

Those moments reminded me that this mission of mine isn't just for me, but for my children, my family, my friends, my network, and for you. To reach and help anyone who decides to read this. Sharing what's helped me build a mindset for success and helping others have the same aha moments is my deeper Why. Seeing the potential for this goal of mine to reach far outside of myself made it impossible for me to ever consider giving up.

FORTIFY YOUR MOTIVATION

Imagine your goal is to run a marathon (26.2 miles), but you're not currently a runner. How likely do you think you are to succeed if you go out every day and attempt the full 26.2 miles? With the exception of very rare humans who can go from zero to 26.2 miles that quick, my bet is on your feeling completely defeated, if not injured, and giving up. Or let's say your goal is to make $100,000 per year, but you currently make $50,000. Unless you are working in a heavy commission role or are at a startup on the brink of huge success and have a big promotion waiting in the wings, it's unlikely to happen in a short period of time, so you need to set micro-goals to track your progress over the length of time you set to achieve it that is realistic for it to take. The further the distance between where you are now and where you want to be, the more you need to arm yourself against feeling defeated or being so full of fear that it's just not going to happen.

If instead you take the time to identify your Whys, you'll find it easier to break up the road to success into smaller achievements that propel you forward with a sense of accomplishment instead of defeat. Perhaps you've identified three Whys for running a marathon:

1. Being able to say you've run a marathon
2. Improving overall fitness and physique
3. Having more energy to play with your kids, nieces or nephews, or other children in your life

With those Whys in mind, it's a lot easier to come up with a plan, such as week-by-week mile achievements that eventually get you to 26.2 miles in time for your marathon, to take regular progress pictures to witness your physical improvements, to dedicate to quality time spent with the children in your life . . . perhaps even including them in your training plans.

As you can discern from above, seeing the ripple effect of your future success as well as having a plan allows you to remain motivated while you work your way up to your goal. And it's a lot less daunting than just having your end goal in your sights. Achievement is a journey and is rarely reached in a single bound. What's better is that these micro-goals don't detract from your end goal, but they do help you to develop the discipline necessary to achieve your end goal.

Discipline is a fantastic companion to faith in the battle with fear, further increasing your odds of reaching success. We'll discuss micro-goals on the road to achievement in more detail in chapter 4, but first I want you to fortify your motivation by building discipline according to your Whys.

Remember when I asked you to dig deeper earlier and answer four questions? Now I want you to consider the sphere of influence you've identified and start to build up even more determination and stick-to-itiveness by answering these follow-up questions:

◊ **What does this accomplishment mean for those I lead and impact?** What will your sphere of influence be able to accomplish, or even just learn, by you following through on this goal? What do you want to teach them? What example are you setting for them?

◊ **Who else will my sphere of influence impact, and how?** Your sphere of influence doesn't end with those impacted by you directly. If they follow your lead and achieve great things that have an impact outside of themselves, the reach of your example continues to expand endlessly. Surely you can think of who inspired you to go for it, meaning you are part of their sphere, and you are likely part of the sphere of the person who inspired them as well. Keep the chain of positive influence going, and consider how far and wide your example can spread.

◊ **What will this achievement allow my community to do next?** It's far easier to give up on something when you only consider the impact on yourself. Once you see even the smallest ways that your hard work and discipline can pay off for countless people, it's too inspiring to give up on. Use that potential for impact to strengthen your resolve and build in you a spirit of perseverance, of discipline.

If discipline is something you struggle with, or if you're having difficulty identifying more than surface-level Whys, I sincerely recommend 75 Hard. A mental toughness program, 75 Hard was created by Andy Frisella. You can learn more on Andy's website,[1] his podcast, RealAF, or in his book *75 Hard: A Tactical Guide to Winning the War with Yourself.*[2]

Between August 2020 and August 2021, I completed Live Hard: the year-long program that begins with seventy-five days of two-a-day workouts, drinking a gallon of water per day, sticking to a diet with no cheats and no alcohol, taking a progress picture daily, and reading ten pages of a nonfiction book daily. After the seventy-five days, there are three thirty-day phases that must be completed before your one-year anniversary of starting 75 Hard. Each of the three thirty-day phases requires at least the same five tasks listed above, while two phases have additional tasks, some of which you set for yourself. Beyond learning the power of micro-goals and seeing massive growth in all areas of my life, the Live Hard program led me to a great appreciation for meditation and visualization (one of the phases requires daily active visualization), as it has for many who've completed the year-long program.

According to the 2017 National Health Interview Survey conducted by the National Center for Complementary and Integrative Health, three times as many people in America are turning to meditation since their survey in 2012 (14.2 percent versus 4.1 percent).[3] Meditation is a tool that can help you in many areas of life, but for our purposes, it can help you identify a deeper meaning to your goals and build discipline on your path to success.

In all honesty, before I discovered my love for meditation, I thought of it as a bit of a hippie/new-age thing that I didn't really identify with at the time. Every year, though, the practice of meditation is becoming more mainstream; in addition to health professionals advocating for its benefits, some of the most successful people you can think of have gotten on board and reaped some amazing benefits, including the late Kobe Bryant, Ellen DeGeneres, Ringo Starr, and Lady Gaga.

Some measurable benefits of meditation include the following:

◊ Meditation improves anxiety levels 60 percent of the time.
◊ Meditation can reduce the risk of being hospitalized for coronary disease by 87 percent.
◊ Meditation can reduce the wake time of people with insomnia by 50 percent, according to mindfulness meditation stats.
◊ Meditation can increase employees' productivity by 120 percent.
◊ School suspensions were reduced by 45 percent thanks to meditation.[4]

In addition to these benefits, I can personally attest to the mental and spiritual clarity that meditation provides. More importantly, meditation is one of the best ways to quiet your negative subconscious.

Consider the thoughts that arise when you look in the mirror or make a mistake or feel overwhelmed with your goal. Are they positive, or do they beat you down? Sadly, these negative thoughts can be so abundant or habitual that you may not even realize their constant jabs from yourself to yourself, or if you want to get really "woo woo," from things you heard as a child that your inner child repeats on a loop. These thoughts become so habitual that you may not even realize you are allowing your conscious and subconscious mind to prevent you from reaching your goals. To this we say, "Hell to the no!"

The first step is starting to recognize these thoughts. If you haven't worked on self-talk, it may feel impossible to stop once you begin to notice just how frequently they arise. Once you do begin to notice them for what they are (think of them as stubborn obstacles standing in the way of the achievement you seek), you can begin the process of flipping them.

> **TIP:** Fixing your mindset on the positive starts with taking each individual thought and molding it into something beneficial. Philippians 4:8 says, "And now, dear brothers and sisters, one final thing. Fix your thoughts on what is true, and honorable, and right, and pure, and lovely, and admirable. Think about things that are excellent and worthy of praise."[5]

Catch yourself mid-mental put-down and switch to a positive thought. If your focus is fitness and you constantly find yourself looking in the mirror criticizing your figure, stop and find one or more things to be grateful for or make a positive note of. If your negative self-talk is self-defeating, such as "I'm not worthy of X" or "I will never be able to Y," stop and come up with a positive. State your inner belief that you *are* worthy and you *can* do whatever you set out to. If you didn't truly believe it, you wouldn't even be trying.

Back to meditation. Another way to combat negative self-talk (a.k.a. achievement killer No. 1) is through the practice of meditation, as it helps in quieting the mind, keeping the negative subconscious thoughts at bay, and allowing you to retrain your conscious and subconscious mind to be more faith than fear-oriented. So, whether you're seeking deeper meaning behind an already established goal or trying to hone in on the right goal to set in this moment, I highly recommend giving meditation a try and sticking to it regularly. You might just become addicted like I have.

There are ample resources for learning how to meditate. The Daily Meditation offers a tutorial on their website.[6] I also recommend searching for guided meditations on YouTube. I personally love the Boho Beautiful Yoga channel and their fourteen-day meditation playlist.[7] If you prefer to do it on your own, here are some steps I've learned that may help you get started:

1. **Find a quiet place, free from distractions.**
2. **Get into a comfortable position.** Depending on your body, you may find that the typical seated position used in meditation is not comfortable for you. If that's the case, lie down or sit in a chair. The important part is to find a position that you can be comfortable in for the duration of your meditation.
3. **Set a timer for the duration you're looking to meditate for to prevent you from stopping to check your watch.** For beginners, five-to-ten minutes should suffice, but you'll find yourself interested in extending the length once you're hooked.
4. **Close your eyes and focus on your breath.** Breath work is the key to meditation. With your eyes closed, inhale deeply through your nose and exhale slowly through your nose or mouth. I've used guided meditations that recommend exhaling through the mouth and others through the nose, but never

any that recommend inhaling through the mouth. After reading *Breath: The New Science of a Lost Art* by James Nestor, I stick to nose breathing, as it's the way our bodies were intended to breathe, with the mouth being a backup method. If you're dealing with congestion or sinus issues, I encourage you to still attempt nose breathing as, surprisingly, it can actually help to reduce congestion.[8] Ultimately, do what's best for you during each meditation session. But if you are a mouth breather, do yourself a favor and read Nestor's book.

5. **Focus on relaxing the mind and body more and more with every exhale.** Visualize the release of any pain, stress, and emotion with each exhale. If you struggle to release your thoughts, go deeper into visualization such as focusing on each body part relaxing one by one or breathing in healing energy to the areas of the body that need it. You can also focus each breath on the release of specific emotions or feelings. All of the above will give you something to focus on other than the thousands of thoughts that may pop up otherwise.

6. **Don't get hung up on the idea of a completely quiet and still mind!** When thoughts arise, visualize them in a cloud and let them drift away. Don't get frustrated when thoughts come up—it's normal. Do return to focusing on your breath, and it will help to slow the train of thought so you can get in the zone.

7. **Set an intention or *sankalpa* (heartfelt desire).** Since we've established that you're working on getting to the root of a goal, identifying a meaningful goal, or simply supporting yourself on the path to achieving a meaningful goal, I suggest creating an affirmation or intention related to that. For example, if you're still trying to identify the goal, your intention could be, "I have a meaningful goal and purpose in my life." If you're working on identifying deeper meaning for an existing goal, "My goal is aligned with my divine life purpose, and I find deep meaning in achieving it." And if you're meditating

to keep you on track, "I achieve my goals for my highest good and the good of others." The key is a present-tense statement, since that is what you are looking to attract. Do not allow fear or doubt to creep into your intention. It will only hinder your progress.

8. **Repeat consistently, ideally daily.** And don't hesitate to adjust your intention. Let your intuition guide you on how it needs to evolve; it does not have to be the same for each meditation.

9. **Thank yourself for doing this important work!**

Now that you've done the work of discovering your deeper purpose and goals, write them down! Putting pen to paper (or finger to laptop?) is a great way to create accountability, as it's something tangible and something you can refer back to when you are struggling or frustrated. While you're at it, jot down milestones as often as possible too. Seeing the unfolding of your success can be a great motivator when you feel like your progress has stalled. And don't you worry, we'll discuss the importance of milestones in just a bit. But first, let's learn to embrace failure, shall we?

3

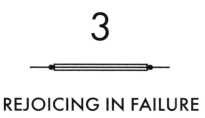

REJOICING IN FAILURE

"We can rejoice, too, when we run into problems and trials, for we know that they help us develop endurance. And endurance develops strength of character, and character strengthens our confident hope of salvation."

ROMANS 5:3–4 (NLT)[1]

You may have read this chapter title and thought, *Yup, she's definitely lost her mind.* But hear me out: failure presents the opportunity to learn, making you that much more likely to succeed on the next try. If you haven't yet read *Mindset: The New Psychology of Success* by Carol Dweck, I highly recommend it. Page after page explains just how impactful a growth mindset—seeing the benefits of failure and learning not to fear it—is to achieving success.[2]

In order to understand which emotions are contributing to our mindset, we have to be able to identify the emotions we are feeling and whether they are moving our mindset in a positive or negative direction. Psychologists have found there are twenty-seven basic human emotions.[3] Famous psychologist Elisabeth Kübler-Ross is known for stating that all human emotion actually stems from just two emotions, love and fear.[4] All positive emotions stem from love, and all negative emotions stem from fear. Here's how I would bucket them:

LOVE

ADMIRATION	INTEREST
ADORATION	JOY
AESTHETIC APPRECIATION	NOSTALGIA
AMUSEMENT	RELIEF
AWE	ROMANCE
CALMNESS	SATISFACTION
EMPATHETIC PAIN	SEXUAL DESIRE
ENTRANCEMENT	SURPRISE
EXCITEMENT	

FEAR

ANGER	CRAVING
ANXIETY	DISGUST
AWKWARDNESS	FEAR
BOREDOM	HORROR
CONFUSION	SADNESS

Figure 3.1. Table displaying emotions grouped under love and fear

Look at those words. Think about the things that elicit those feelings for you and then think about how they can be summed up to a feeling of love versus fear. I'm not suggesting that anyone should eliminate all feelings in the fear category or never feel them; that would be impossible, and you'd miss the opportunity to use them as the powerful tools they can be. But when you are chasing a dream, think about which, if any, of those in the fear category can still help you move forward—even when you don't squeeze the good or learning out of them. If anything, we can all learn a lesson from Steve Jobs on how to leverage those negative emotions and turn them into motivation to succeed.

As you likely know, Steve Jobs cofounded Apple Computer (now Apple Inc.) in 1976 at just twenty-one years old. By twenty-three, he was a millionaire. Sounds like your standard Silicon Valley success story, right? Wrong.

Over the years, internal disputes led to Jobs getting fired from the company he'd built that had made him a legend and a multimillionaire. At thirty years old (1985), he was shoved out and devastated. He immediately began working on some new ventures that you may have heard of: a new computer company called NeXT and Pixar Animation Studio. In 1996, Apple acquired NeXT, and Jobs returned a year later.[5] In a speech to Stanford University graduates, Jobs had this to say about the experience.

"I didn't see it then, but it turned out that getting fired from Apple was the best thing that could have ever happened to me. The heaviness of being successful was replaced by the lightness of being a beginner again, less sure about everything. It freed me to enter into one of the most creative periods of my life . . .

"I'm pretty sure none of this would have happened if I hadn't been fired from Apple. It was awful tasting medicine, but I guess the patient needed it. Sometimes life hits you in the head with a brick. Don't lose faith. I'm convinced the only thing that kept me going was that I loved what I did. You've got to find what you love."

—STEVE JOBS[6]

As I reflect on my own career, I can relate to the heaviness of success that Jobs spoke of in his speech. For every rung on the ladder I climbed, I faced a new mountain of doubt. Numerous times, I allowed that doubt and fear to creep in and felt like I surely couldn't succeed. And time and time again, once I gathered my faith (shout out to my hubby for always being quick to lift my confidence by having faith in me!), I found myself succeeding at what I falsely believed I couldn't do and then moving on to a new challenge.

While I appreciate and feel blessed by my rapid career growth, it was definitely challenging. Presenting performance metrics for my team was something I'd longed to be responsible for in previous roles; I've always been a little bit of a data nerd. I learned very quickly during my time at ZipRecruiter that there's a big difference in both reporting on a small team versus a large team and presenting to a small group of executives versus a room full of seasoned executives and a full C-suite. I've never had a fear of public speaking; in fact, I took a public speaking course in college just so that I could have more opportunities to do it . . . and I loved it. Let me tell you, I was not expecting this thing we call anxiety to suddenly make an appearance during my presentation prep, causing me to revise the presentation time and time again, or to feel the need to second-guess that I did in fact know how to do math. Nor did I know where the shaky voice and sweaty palms came from when I found myself standing up in the conference room surrounded by a sea of executives—all of whom had years, if not decades, more experience—and at larger companies—than me.

Thankfully, that first presentation went smoothly, alleviating my fears that I'd suddenly forgotten how to do the math I'd always done for my own understanding of how I or my team was performing. That's not to say all presentations went smoothly. I'll never forget presenting plans for tackling account churn (i.e., how to prevent accounts/clients from cancelling service), thinking I'd nailed what the C-suite was looking for and that I'd used the right data to run my calculations and form my plans.

After the last slide, I was beaming with pride; then came the feeling of defeat when I learned I'd gone in the wrong direction and accidentally used the wrong set of data to form my plans to attack churn. My initial reaction was to blame the messenger, but that wasn't productive. Instead, I made a mental note to repeat back anything that was asked of me and verify that the way I planned on gathering the necessary data was correct, instead of being so eager to please and run off on a mission I didn't fully understand. Despite an initial fear that asking these questions would make me look like an idiot, I was always met with clarity and, at times, helped leadership to see that the way they made requests could be confusing and lead those of us acting on these requests on a wild goose chase.

That said, the repetition of these experiences in a relatively short span of time helped me to grow accustomed to the flow of using fear as a tool: gaining confidence, growing, and starting all over again.

I've often been referred to as a change agent, and I'm not one who typically dreads change—I'm generally all for it. But when changes—or, really, growth opportunities—present you with the unknown, it can be easy for fear to take hold. Maybe it's as simple as not knowing how to do something you are now expected to do. Maybe it's fear that you'll fail and there will be a consequence. Maybe it's just fear that some deep-seated belief that you aren't good enough will actually come true. The trick is to tap into what you *love* about what you're doing and learn to appreciate the challenges, obstacles, and setbacks for how they reaffirm your passion for whatever it is you are doing.

LEARN TO LOVE THE PROCESS

We've all experienced growing pains—physically, mentally, spiritu-ally . . . Growth in any sense is never easy. It can be painful. It can be frustrating. It can make you question your Whys. But if you can see beyond that temporary pain and appreciate that process, you'll be able to tap into a success mindset and train yourself to love that process, no matter how uncomfortable, for the blessings it brings. Here are some things to consider during those painful growth spurts:

◊ Identify the pain you're feeling, whether it's physical, mental, spiritual, financial, or emotional.

◊ What is on the other side of this pain? What *could* be on the other side of that pain? Tap into what will come when you get through it. That focus will make enduring whatever pain you're feeling easier to withstand, and you'll be there before you know it.

◊ How long do you realistically think the pain will last?

◊ Are there better ways to cope with the pain?

◊ Are there different strategies you can attempt to work your way through the pain to get to the other side sooner?

◊ What is this period of discomfort teaching you?

Each challenging time we encounter is an opportunity for growth. Simply sitting in the discomfort and only recognizing the lack or the pain we feel doesn't move us forward. It gives us nothing to study up for, to prepare for, and that's not a fun or productive place to be. If you can see the learning opportunity in the midst of your pain, you'll be more likely to take a student approach and use this uncomfortable period to study up and be that much more ready for what comes after.

For many women and minority groups who don't have equal representation in their industry or role, tackling that fear and gaining confidence is such an important process. If I haven't clearly explained this yet, let me tell you that learning to be confident in business has been a struggle for me. It took me years to learn and understand that what I was feeling was primarily imposter syndrome. Not only was I often the youngest executive in the room, but also quite often the only woman, or one of few. I was also generally the one with the least executive or even overall professional experience.

Throughout my career, I've seen the shock on many people's faces—from leaders to colleagues to clients—when their assumption that I was low on the totem pole due to my age was squashed by learning that I was actually an executive. At times, as I've described, recognizing that I was the least experienced (and/or one of the only women) in the room generated fear for me. I've always enjoyed the shock value of showing people I can do something they don't expect or assume; sometimes I enjoyed the lack of expectations and my ability to impress by often having a better grasp of data or the business than even they, with all their years of experience, had. What I did not enjoy, however, were the patronizing remarks about how I was so young to be at my level. Those experiences were part of why I decided to be a champion for diversity, equity, and inclusion in whatever way I could.

It's not uncommon to experience conscious or unconscious bias in the workplace or even our day-to-day lives, and those experiences of feeling invisible, overlooked, and undervalued can create unconscious beliefs about our abilities.

Kelly Shue from the Yale School of Management, Alan Benson from the University of Minnesota, and Danielle Li from Massachusetts Institute of Technology (MIT) coauthored a study in 2021 that showed women are 14 percent less likely to be promoted each year. The study dives into the bias that exists in performance assessments leading to this delta, creating a funnel wherein women represent the majority of employees in entry-level roles and that representation gets smaller and smaller at each progressive job level.[7]

Couple this data with the unconscious beliefs I just mentioned, and it's easy to see why, on average, women and minority groups tend to hold off on requesting raises, promotions, or even from personally attempting to tackle a new challenge until they are 100 percent sure they can do it without any doubt. And if we're not careful, we can sit on this truth and let ourselves be overcome with many of the emotions in the fear category, rightly feeling upset by the inequality we face. We aren't going to get anywhere by simply being upset about these truths. There are actions we can and should, I would say *must*, take.

The problem with holding back is you miss the opportunity to get into a flow with facing doubt, growing your confidence, and believing you have what it takes to move to the next level. While systems and workplaces do need to address the vast amount of conscious and unconscious bias that exists, I believe every one of us needs to do the same internally. Again, the experience of bias often creates an internal unconscious bias that holds you back. The more you work to confront and overcome those biases within, the more you'll put yourself out there. Will you risk failure? Absolutely! But will it be worth it? Again, absolutely! Let's take a look at Oprah Winfrey for some inspiration.

The Oprah Winfrey Show had been No. 1 in its spot for more than two decades when Oprah decided it was time to jump into a new challenge and create the Oprah Winfrey Network (OWN). From the average person's vantage point, it seemed like a layup for her. Wrong.

A year after launching OWN, she woke up to headlines claiming the network was a flop. In a 2013 Harvard University commencement speech, this is what she had to say about the experience:

"It really was, this time last year, the worst period in my professional life. I was stressed and I was frustrated, and quite frankly I was—actually I was embarrassed . . . And the words came to me, 'Trouble don't last always,' from that hymn, 'This Too Shall Pass.' And I thought . . . I am going to turn this thing around, and I will be better for it. . . . So I'm here today to tell you I have turned that network around!"

—Oprah Winfrey [8]

It's easy to think that the climb is the difficult part, especially when your climb is admittedly more difficult than others, but success has a way of constantly challenging you and forcing you to continue to grow. If we let ourselves believe that success or achieving some milestone means we are done, we're kidding ourselves. Perhaps that's why you're reading this book. Success is heavy. It brings with it greater responsibility, greater desire for growth, and failures that we must endure and learn from along the way.

How does the idea of failure make you feel? Try reprogramming your response to the thought of failure, even if you have to fake it until it comes naturally to you. Remind yourself that there's something to learn and an opportunity to grow as a result of each and every failure. Eventually, you will learn to embrace both fear and failure and use them to fuel your motivation and discipline. More than that, once you've reprogrammed yourself to love failure, you'll be more willing to try. Logically, you know that you can't win if you don't try. When fear creeps in, the anticipated consequences prevent you from putting yourself out there. So again, I say, "Rejoice in failure."

I've read many books about finding your purpose and achieving success. Between the stories in those books and the successful people I've witnessed and interviewed along with my own experiences with success, there's a common thread that leads to achieving success: failure, or, rather, not being afraid to fail and seeing the opportunities that failure presents. In *The Luck Factor: Four Simple Principles that Will Change Your Luck—and Your Life* by Dr. Richard Wiseman, you'll find data to confirm this fact.[9] The more you fear failure, the less you make attempts at whatever you're looking to succeed at, and, thus, the less "lucky" you are. In reality, this thing we call "luck" is just a result of your mindset. Believe you are lucky, go after The Thing as many times as it takes, and you'll eventually succeed.

In whatever situation you find yourself right now, what are you expecting God to do? Are you expecting Him to do anything? If you're not, remember that God works in your life according to your expectation. That's called faith!

RESHAPE FEAR

"If you don't try at anything, you can't fail . . .
it takes backbone to lead the life you want."
—RICHARD YATES[10]

"There is only one thing that makes a dream
impossible to achieve: the fear of failure."
—PAULO COELHO[11]

These two quotes, along with the "Control Your Emotions" chapter in Ryan Holiday's book *The Obstacle Is the Way: The Timeless Art of Turning Trials into Triumph*, remind me of a lesson my dad taught me as a child. One particular experience comes to mind: my first C on a test. I was a straight-A student, and after being out of school for a couple of weeks due to strep throat, I returned to take a test I wasn't prepared for and got a C. I was devastated. (You can laugh, I do now.)

My dad was trying to get me to shake it off and asked me if the world was going to end today because of that grade. Through sobs, I stubbornly answered no. That was the reset I needed to realize that as big as that C felt, it really wasn't a big deal. In *The Obstacle Is the Way*, Holiday uses similar examples that can be applied to adult situations, business, etc. But in one particular section, he encourages readers to ask a similar question, "Am I going to die?", and then to continue to remind yourself that you aren't, in fact, going to die because of a business hiccup or unfortunate situation. This realization is key to moving on from the natural and strong emotions we feel when it comes to failure—whether it's just our perception that we've failed or not, and instead move into a spirit of resourcefulness, which is far more productive.[12]

Joyce Meyer so clearly explains that difficulty in itself is not a guarantee of growth. Regardless of the inequality we may be faced with, we still must adopt a student mindset and seek to learn through each difficulty. This means setting aside, or rather putting, our fear-category emotions to good use.

> *"We do not grow or become strong during life's good times;*
> *we grow when we press through difficulties without giving up.*
> *Growth is not an automatic result of difficulty. Hardships do not*
> *necessarily produce growth or strength in us; it is not that simple.*
> *We must choose the right attitude toward our challenges and refuse*
> *to quit or give up. We may have to do what is right for a long time*
> *before we feel it is 'paying off,' but if we stay faithful and refuse*

to give up, good results will come. Once we get through the adversity and challenges we face, we emerge as better people than we were when we went into them."

—JOYCE MEYER, TRUSTING GOD DAY BY DAY[13]

However you must reshape those fear emotions, craft them into the tools you need to power through each difficulty with your eye on the lesson, the learning, and the opportunity it's presenting to you. Without those tools, you've simply experienced and endured difficulty. With them, you've conquered those challenges. Which would you prefer? Ask yourself which situation will feel more empowering.

Going back to your notepad or Google doc tracking your goal and progress, include your failures *and* learnings from them. Pay homage to the failures you experience for the growth they allow you to capture. The most difficult thing to deal with when it comes to failure is admitting any error or misstep. But honestly, who's judging you? Primarily yourself. It's similar to the natural defensive response we feel when criticized. My thought on failure and criticism is *Bring it on, it can only make me better.* I encourage you to adopt a similar response.

4

———◆━━━━◆———

CELEBRATING THE MILESTONES

In order to notice the milestones, you've got to take the time to check in on your progress. Setting micro-goals is a helpful way to ensure this happens. Facing down one gigantic goal is a lot. Seeing a roadmap of progress and mini-milestones that get you there is much easier to wrap your brain around. There's actual science to back up the benefits of celebrating wins.

Did you know that winning or feeling a sense of accomplishment stimulates dopamine, serotonin, and oxytocin?[1] Think of these as the happy chemicals inside your brain. The more you experience the feeling of winning or reward from your efforts, the more your brain seeks ways to repeat those happy feelings. So instead of constantly being hard on yourself, if you make it a point to set micro-goals that keep you on pace to achieve your goal, you'll not only be well on your way to success, but you'll also be fortifying your motivation and creating the discipline—and chemical reactions inside your brain—that deepen your commitment to doing it again and again and again, creating some incredibly powerful habits.

Acknowledging even the smallest win can give your faith and discipline a boost when motivation fades and you're staring at yet *another* steep climb toward your end goal. Ever heard of the saying, "Progress, not perfection"? This is incredibly wise advice. If you're only ever focused on perfection, you allow worry or fear to creep in, focusing on potential criticisms you could receive or failures you could endure and miss the opportunity to put your hat in the ring.

Look around you. Are you being surpassed by people who aren't so focused on perfection? Are your peers or colleagues moving ahead while you're heads-down clawing at perfection? If so, it might be time to adjust your bar for what you need to accomplish before taking the next step. What's the worst that could happen? You could fail. If so, see chapter 3 on why that's a great way to get ahead! When you focus on progress—and celebrate that progress—instead of narrowing in on perfection, you gain momentum. It doesn't matter how minor the progress might be, honoring it and celebrating it can be a tool to prevent fear from slowing you down. Thomas Edison said it well:

> *"Many of life's failures are people who did not realize how close they were to success when they gave up."*
>
> —THOMAS EDISON[2]

If you're part of an underrepresented group, you may identify with the idea of focusing on perfection: you're ambitious and working hard at all the right things, yet noticing others around you move to the next level without seeming to toil quite as hard. This isn't a message to despise them, but perhaps we can learn something from them. Again, let's focus on progress, not perfection, and identify whether we are too focused on checking every box instead of working hard and seeking out the opportunity to progress—even if there are still some boxes left to check.

When we focus so rigidly on meeting, or surpassing, every single requirement we think is needed to get to the next level in whatever it is we are seeking, we may well miss an opportunity that arises when we assume we aren't quite ready—especially in the workforce. Promotions don't come every day. And for every opportunity that arises that we decide not to throw our hat in the ring for because we think we're not quite ready yet, there are many others who will take that chance and get it. Observing others who aren't quite ready receive the opportunity we are working so hard for can be disheartening. It can actually push you further into perfection mode.

Are there times when someone will step in and give you that shot in recognition of your hard work and capabilities? Absolutely. But we are the masters of our own destiny and must find ways to carve the path for ourselves. This means not holding back. It means not waiting for someone to come along and make it happen for us. Seek advice and mentorship (yes, by all means). Explore the situations in which you've felt passed over. Discover whether you were in fact passed over, or if you simply didn't raise your hand to be considered. I say all this because underrepresented groups tend to do less hand raising because we fear rejection more. We put more pressure on ourselves to be perfect in order to succeed, and, sadly, it often holds us back, further adding to our conclusion that we must work that much harder and be that much more "perfect" to succeed. This is not the case.

Despite growing up with the phrase "practice makes perfect," my brain's default managed to focus on stepping stones when it came to achieving goals instead of the giant leaps one might imagine when thinking about reaching perfection. My outspoken nature and inability to stop asking questions, such as "Hasn't my role changed?" or "Do my new responsibilities come with a raise?" served me well in finding ways to get to the next stepping stone. That's not to say I never felt passed over. Early in my career, there were certainly times I felt like waving my arms saying, "Hellooooo. I'm right here. What about me?!" I tended to deal with those situations internally and found a way to make my own next step, often at a new job. While those transitions felt like success to me, it was a lonely journey.

Once I was in a leadership position, I noticed pretty quickly that there was a distinct difference in who would come to me with ideas about the next step in their career or pay level. I'll give you a hint, it generally wasn't the women or minorities who were on my team. That realization changed my leadership style—and for the better.

I began to conduct what I call Reset One-on-Ones with every member of my team. Regardless of how long they'd been working for me, I started back at square one and asked them questions about their personal and professional goals. With some employees, these questions opened the floodgates; others needed time to sit on the question and think about how to identify their goals. Many of the women and minorities I led had incorrect assumptions about how long it would take them to get to their next step, or if it was even possible, thinking there was a hard-and-fast timeline or that they had to perfect everything from A to Z. I was more than happy to tell them how wrong those assumptions could be.

In all cases, I eventually got an answer and was able to coach them on ways to achieve their goals, and find side projects to build the skills they needed for their next step, and many of them achieved the goals they set during my time leading them. This was yet another experience that made me realize (a) how fulfilling being a growth-focused leader was, and (b) how disheartening it could be for an employee to work for a leader who didn't bother to push their employees to identify goals and coach them toward achieving them. I remembered how lonely it was for me, and I continued to find ways to eliminate the solo hustle for as many people as I could by opening my door to any and every employee, friend, and industry contact who needed advice or a little push to set goals for themselves.

A friend, mentor, and badass female leader I know, Leah Daniels, once dropped this wisdom on me in reference to people she's led: "When you make yourself irreplaceable, you make yourself unpromotable." The idea of being irreplaceable is enticing for people who want to ensure job security, but it works against you if your goal is to grow beyond where you are. What boss in their right mind is going to promote someone out of a job that no one else can do? The answer is few, if any.

If you find yourself in this situation currently, look around you and identify people whose next step would be your job. Can you work with them to learn the elements of your role that only you can do at this moment? If you can't see anyone to transfer that knowledge to, start documenting. If you can produce step-by-step guides on how to do your role as efficiently as you do it, you're moving in the right direction.

One of the best ways I've found as a leader to promote growth at all levels is a shared team playbook. Given my work with startups, the playbook has always started with me in defining the roles I planned to build out on my teams and each of their responsibilities. From there, I'd outline the most common scenarios or tasks the roles would be dealing with and outline step-by-step how to handle the situation or complete the task effectively. Once I had people in those roles, starting from their first week in training, I'd turn the playbook over to them. In my experience, there is no one better than a new hire to revise the processes outlined in a playbook. Why? Because they haven't yet adopted shorthand and are looking for clear ways to handle their tasks on their own. Over time, all members of the team recognize the time saved using this valuable tool, as it enables everyone on the team, new or old, to work independently and find the answers to most of their questions.

Whether or not your current team has anything resembling this kind of playbook, if you're feeling stuck and think you're falling into the irreplaceable/unpromotable trap, get started on transferring your knowledge so you can escape the trap. This is a measurable milestone, and could be a micro-goal if your ultimate goal is to get promoted or work your way up in your company.

MICRO-GOALS

The US Navy SEALs are often credited with coining the term "micro-goals," as it's something they employ to get through Hell Week. If it works for the navy SEALs, I'm certain it will work for you. Here are some ways to get started on creating your micro-goals:

1. **Start with your end goal.** Set a date that you'd like to complete it.

2. **Map out your micro-goals.** Working backward from that ultimate completion date, chart a course to hit those micro-goals that lead to your ultimate goal attainment.[3]

3. **Spend some time thinking about the daily activities you need to accomplish to reach each short-term, or micro-goal, then add them to a daily task list.** Use the medium that works best for you to do this. Some people like writing task lists down with pen and paper, others (like me) work better in a spreadsheet. It doesn't matter how you write them down, but it's important that you do, or you are less likely to stay accountable to the work that needs to be done daily to get you to each milestone and your end goal.

4. **Find an accountability partner.** Another accountability hack is to share those daily commitments with your partner or support system. It's one thing to commit to them yourself, but once you share it with others, you will be more likely to stay true to them.

5. **Review your progress consistently, and add or adjust the daily tasks that will keep you on track to your end goal.** Do expect some backslides or times when you feel you've taken one step forward and two steps back. Don't beat yourself up over those times. Instead, think of the rubber band theory, which says that those times we feel we've moved backward are often followed by being propelled forward. Embrace those slingshot moments, even if it's as simple as recognizing the new paths forward that can be discovered when you've inadvertently taken a few steps back. Perspective is key.

In my experience, people either love or hate task lists. If you are in the latter camp, don't brush off this advice. Give it a shot. Think of it as motivational armor. The more often you are able to reward your brain with the happy chemicals of dopamine, serotonin, and oxytocin, the more motivated you'll be—which eventually transforms into a dedicated discipline that makes you an unstoppable, goal-getting machine.

If you're finding it difficult to complete the daily tasks you've set for yourself and can't seem to get out of the cycle of skipping them, then beating yourself up about it, revise your list! Again, like the marathon example I gave, you have to meet yourself where you are and work your way up to where you need to be. If you're like me, you might overfill your plate and take on too much too quickly, then burn out. (Been there, done that far too many times.) To get out of either cycle, you've got to reevaluate your expectations and likely start smaller.

During my 75 Hard journey, I learned how to overcome my cycle of burnout and feeling frustrated. While I knew what I was attempting to accomplish each day were all the "right" things, I was simply starting from an unrealistic place and hadn't developed the discipline or mindset to continue at that pace just yet.

In Phase 1 of Live Hard, you're required to do ten minutes of active visualization every day. At first, I laughed at this task, thinking surely this isn't going to do anything for me. I'm not ashamed to admit how very wrong I was. This micro-of-all-microtasks opened my eyes to the power of small wins . . . and the beauty of visualization. The sense of accomplishment I felt being able to check this additional task off my list each day gave me an idea.

When it came time to start Phase 2 of Live Hard, in which you have to come up with some additional tasks that are intended to move you forward in any way, I decided it was time to stop living in the "some days," as I knew my opportunity for retirement was approaching.

This book started with a microtask I also laughed at initially: writing or even just thinking about and researching what I wanted to do upon retirement for fifteen minutes a day. There were days that I did fifteen minutes and that was it—task completed. There were also many days when I spent significantly more time on developing ideas for my passion project despite having been a habitual "I don't have enough time" type of person. Within days, I had my "duh" moment: I'd always wanted to be an author and spread inspiration to remind others of their amazing potential and ability to succeed at whatever it is they feel passionate about. That laughable fifteen minutes a day is how this book was born. Over time, it became easier to stick to the habit of committing to small amounts of progress every day, which helped get me over writer's block humps or feeling stuck in any way.

MOTIVATION BEFORE DISCIPLINE

The point is there is nothing wrong with starting small—even so small that you want to laugh at how meaningless it may seem. Consistently making even the smallest amount of progress triggers all those happy chemicals in your brain and trains your discipline muscles. Don't believe me? Check out *The Procrastination Equation: How to Stop Putting Things Off and Start Getting Stuff Done* by Piers Steel, PhD. A professor of organizational dynamics, Steel believes that motivation can be understood as an equation:[4]

$$\text{MOTIVATION} = \frac{\text{EXPECTANCY} \times \text{VALUE}}{\text{IMPULSIVENESS} \times \text{DELAY}}$$

Figure 4.1. Equation for Motivation

As much as I may harp on discipline being the ultimate rainmaker for success, motivation is required to get the ball rolling. Motivation can be fleeting, but it's the jumping-off point to developing the necessary discipline to achieve your goals. Without it, you wind up twiddling your thumbs and getting stuck in the Some Day cycle, looking forward but never taking a step toward that future.

Let's dive into Steel's motivation equation . . .

Expectancy is the belief you hold about the outcome of the work you're doing. When you believe there will be a negative or less-than-positive outcome, you're more likely to procrastinate. Why would you invest time and energy on something you're not expecting to generate a win, or at least something positive and rewarding? When you control your mindset and find ways to create a positive expectation, you will be less likely to procrastinate. When you believe that you can achieve the milestone and something good will come from it, you will also decrease your impulsivity and delays, thus putting you on a better path to completing the milestone or objective you've set for yourself.

One simple way to hack this shift in perspective is to identify a reward you give yourself if there is unlikely to be a natural reward for the work you're doing. While I'm not the biggest fan of food rewards, perhaps you establish a pattern where you get to eat your favorite fruit. Or read a fun book or grant yourself some other harmless guilty pleasure for an allotted time when you complete your fifteen-minute task. Giving yourself something to look forward to after marking the task as complete each day is a great motivator.

Value is all about focusing on the work, not the outcome. Sounds weird for a milestone, but as outcomes aren't under your control and your effort is, it works better to activate motivation. If you can keep yourself focused on the value you expect to get out of completing your tasks, your motivation will only be stronger. If you don't get enjoyment out of what you're doing, you are more likely to procrastinate.

There are less than enjoyable aspects to just about any goal journey, but if you can hack your mindset to find something to enjoy, even if it's your self-delivered reward, you will overcome the natural detours into impulsivity and delays, which only leave you standing further from your end goal and likely frustrated or feeling defeated.

All of this to say, you are in control of your perspective. Perspective and mindfully adjusting said perspective are key to building the habits and discipline needed to achieve any goal. To create a habit, you need to establish a cue to trigger your brain into motivation mode, a routine to keep you on track, and a reward to reinforce the value of the routines you're creating.

Focus on progress over perfection, create micro-goals, and focus on the value of those micro-goals, and you'll be well on your way to establishing the motivation and discipline needed to succeed mightily in your goal.

> **TIP:** Take the time to map out the milestones that will get you to your end goal. Within each of those milestones, define the microtasks that are necessary to reaching each milestone. Start as small as you need to so you don't burn out and can continuously establish the habits and discipline that will allow you to gain momentum as you move through each milestone.

5

———————————

LEADING YOURSELF FIRST

If you're reading and applying the concepts I've outlined, you've been on a journey to (1) set a meaningful goal and dig deep into the Why to keep your motivation engine running, (2) learning to develop discipline and the importance of viewing failure as an opportunity, and (3) celebrating your wins while consistently self-reflecting, identifying micro-goals to keep you progressing toward success, and letting your intuition/God/the Universe guide you through your overall journey. Now, let's talk about doing the work when it comes to leading yourself toward success, not just at work, but in every area of your life.

While I always recommend finding a mentor and support system, it's not going to do much good if you're not Leading Yourself First down the path to success. You can't take a backseat on your own journey; it has to start with you sitting in the driver's seat. And let's face it: if you're not the primary driver, your support system is going to lose interest in helping you along the way. As I look back at my life, I realize that, while sports had a profound impact on teaching me so many life lessons—time management, character, teamwork, leadership—I grew a little too accustomed to the structure and direction I received from my coaches. It didn't hit me until I went off to college.

Due to a shoulder injury and opting out of surgery, I decided not to play water polo even though I had an opportunity to redshirt my freshman year and be the starting goalie the following year. Instead, I decided to get a job to support my end of the finances my parents and I had agreed upon. Without the consistent (and intense) workout schedule I'd been used to for over four years, and with an In-n-Out around the corner from my college campus, I quickly gained the Freshman 15 (more like twenty, but who's counting?).

For the first time since my "awkward phase" around ten years old, I suddenly felt uncomfortable in my clothes; the stomach I'd kept flat and toned was nowhere to be found. That's when it hit me. I no longer had a coach to push me to swim lap upon lap, hit the weight room, or even (my least favorite) go for a run. Not working out consistently and not eating a balanced diet certainly wasn't working. It didn't take long for me to jump in the driver's seat and take control of my health and physique. And yes, even run.

At the time, my dad and older brother were into bodybuilding, so I sought advice from them on workout routines and a healthy diet to help me achieve my goals. They encouraged me, and often laughed when I got frustrated by the sheer volume of chicken I was forcing myself to eat. We still laugh about my outburst one day that "It's all frickin' chicken!"

I will tell you that it was infinitely more fulfilling to achieve those goals because I decided to push myself instead of relying on someone else to tell me what to do. And it certainly helped to have a like-minded support system during my moments of weakness, a.k.a. chicken-gate.

It all starts with the self. Had I sought help from my family but not actually acted on their advice, it wouldn't have been long before they stopped offering it. Your commitment and passion for reaching your destination is key to helping you overcome the many obstacles that will appear, and it will inspire others to give you the support and help you need.

In order to maintain the discipline and motivation that are so important in achieving your goals, you must know how to do two things: (1) lead yourself with faith and confidence, and (2) recognize leadership styles of others around you. Knowing what types of leaders you are dealing with in your everyday life—whether at work, in social spheres, or even with family—will provide insight into their thought processes and give you the ability to change your mindset and take control in situations when you may otherwise have felt in the dark. High self-confidence is one of the keys to motivation, which drives discipline in turn.

I initially thought I was going to write this book to help leaders step up their game. Then I realized I could help significantly more people if I wrote to *you* and helped *you* find *your* inner leader and make that drastic impact *yourself.* In my heart of hearts, I am someone who simply wants to help; I'm also a logical problem solver. When it comes to the professional environment, it saddens me to report that many leaders—especially those new to leadership—have such drive and potential to be transformational leaders, but they lack training, support, inspiring mentors, and often emotional intelligence. What saddens me more is the number of people whose lives would change drastically for the better if they just had some time with an invested, emotionally intelligent leader who could help them see their potential. This book is a tool that I hope you will use to recognize your own potential for success as well as open the door for further mentoring and coaching, if that is something you desire.

OWN YOUR EXPERIENCE

> *"It doesn't matter who you are, where you came from. The ability to triumph begins with you. Always, always."*
>
> —OPRAH WINFREY[1]

Throughout these pages, I've introduced ideas and tips to help you own your experiences in life and use them for your growth. For your success. For your future.

I'd like to switch gears a little bit and dive into the state of leadership in business, leadership styles, how to identify a leadership style, and (of course) how to leverage each style for your growth and to improve your experience at work as a leader, employee, and a human being. Why? Because you will find attributes of some or many of these leadership styles in yourself and those around you, all of which can be applied to leadership in all areas of life, not just work. Identifying attributes of leadership styles and knowing how those styles differ from each other can help you control any situation you are in by reflecting them from the leader's perspective.

Seeing as work takes up the lion's share of our daily lives, I think it's an important area to spend some time discussing. Being able to identify the styles of those you interact with or rely on for support can eliminate the frustration you may feel in not getting the support or leadership you desire, and thus put you back into the driver's seat, feeling a sense of control over your destiny *even* when you're dealing with a boss who can seem more like a roadblock. The goal is to feel empowered, not helpless, regardless of your situation.

First, I want to establish the importance of bringing the whole self to everything that you do. I've always found it odd that so many people put such effort into separating their work persona from their personal persona. You are still you—whether you're at home, work, the gym, church, or the grocery store. At work, there seems to be the biggest expectation of separating the "real" you from the professional you. Again, most people typically spend a good chunk of their time at work, so why not seek to incorporate the whole you *and* aim for a pleasant experience as humans when it comes to work?

When I first stepped into a formal leadership position in business, having just received human resources training, I'm not afraid to admit I felt as though I had to always be my business self at work. It didn't take me long to figure out that wasn't a great way to connect with the members of my team. I find it a blessing that my first team consisted of a lot of people early on in their careers, primarily because they hadn't yet adopted a business identity over a personal one. They were a great example of bringing your whole self to work and frankly a guide for me making the shift.

Realizing that many of them needed not just a business coach, but someone who understood who they were as a whole helped me to share more of myself, setting an example and declaring our conversations as a safe space to be as open as they were comfortable with. I was relieved to find that the more they learned about the whole me, the more connected they felt to me and the more comfortable they felt coming to me for advice on things that were affecting them at work, whether business or personal. I would often have heart-to-hearts with my employees about topics not at all related to work; if they needed an ear, I was more than happy to supply it. As a leader, understanding all aspects of my employees allowed me to lead them in the ways they needed as individuals. Had I not been an open book and related to them when they shared personal situations, I doubt I would have gotten the insights I needed to be the best leader I could be for them.

There are many people talking about the Great Resignation in the wake of the COVID-19 pandemic. If you ask me, I think it's really more of an awakening. During the pandemic shutdowns, a large portion of the American workforce shifted to working remotely, making it nearly impossible to separate their personal identities from their professional lives and personalities. In my opinion, this experience has led to many of those people realizing what their work/life balance actually looks like, and many people are setting new boundaries on what they will tolerate when it comes to that balance. To that I say, "Hallelujah!"

I also believe that many people are realizing we spend far too much time at work to not enjoy it, get fulfillment from it, and simply feel good about the work we're doing. I believe the key to improving all of the above comes down to leadership—self leadership in standing up for what you will and won't tolerate, and business leadership in recognizing that you can't expect people to stay in a thankless, stressful job for decades or even to remain committed to the company's goals if you aren't supporting their personal and professional goals.

All too often, companies—or, rather, those at the top of many companies—seem to promote the idea that leaders are to be listened to and not questioned, feared, and respected regardless of whether there is anything respectable about the leader. Often, it seems the least respectable leaders demand the most respect, causing most of us to respond by throwing our hands in the air and wanting to give up on the idea that we can have anything but a terrible, no-good hypocrite for a boss.

This misguided perception of how to work with leadership is similar to the "children are to be seen and not heard" thinking of days gone by. I think we can all agree that both concepts are outdated. As a parent, I cannot imagine a world where my children don't express themselves. Yes, it's loud. I have three children, and I'm certain there is some mathematical formula that explains how the noise level increases exponentially with each additional child, but there are just so many incredible opportunities for learning when people who are not in positions of power or authority (i.e., children and employees) feel welcome to share their thoughts and opinions. I've seen my children understand and master concepts that seem foreign to many adults when it comes to communication and relationships with others—something my husband and I attribute to our open dialogue with our children. I've always applied the same basic thought to leading employees, and it's resulted in amazing input from my employees, growth for them and for me, and some pretty amazing relationships.

Before I introduce five popular leadership styles and talk about how to recognize and work with different types of leaders, let's look at employee engagement. Maximizing your engagement at work—as either a leader or an employee—can drive your dedication and enrich your day-to-day life, helping to build confidence, rather than fear, in all you do.

LEARNINGS FOR ALL LEADERS

Based on the responses from Qualtrics's 2020 Global Employee Experience Survey, below are the key elements that contribute to employee engagement, a key benchmark in the productivity and satisfaction of the workforce. I'll expand on each of these elements and how you as a leader can improve any one (or all) of these metrics.

If you are an employee, reflect on which of these elements drives your own engagement.

What drives employee engagement?

1. Confidence in senior leadership to make the right decisions for the company (53 percent)
2. Opportunities for learning and development (60 percent)
3. A clear link between your work and the company's strategic objectives (57 percent)
4. Recognition for good work (55 percent)
5. Managers who help employees with career development (50 percent)[2]

1. Confidence in Senior Leadership

Demonstrating an unwavering moral compass and integrity allows your employees to trust that you will always make the right decision, regardless of the circumstances. During the COVID-19 global pandemic in early 2020, I had the opportunity to work with leaders who were immovable in their mission to make the right decisions not only for the company but also for its employees. We were able to weather the economic storms that surged from the pandemic without a single layoff. In fact, multiple senior level executives took pay cuts to ensure that commitment could be reality. They did so without announcement, fanfare, or the majority of the staff even knowing what they had done.

It's in these types of situations, unprecedented or not, that all eyes are pointed directly at those in power. Work to ensure you and your leadership team think carefully about the right thing to do.

2. Opportunities for Learning and Development

One of my biggest personal frustrations with many leaders and managers is the lack of effort spent on learning and development for their employees. If you're following at least the basic tenets of management 101, you believe in conducting regular one-on-ones with your team. If you don't, let's pretend that you do, and question why you don't just make that happen because that's a huge gap if you aren't doing that currently.

Where many leaders go wrong is they apply a selfish or urgent my-questions-matter-more attitude when it comes to one-on-ones. These meetings can easily become a grilling session where they're just firing away at your report demanding answers, giving warnings, or otherwise crossing off their HR checklist to make sure any and all performance issues are made clear as well as the consequences if another instance should occur. While, yes, a one-on-one is an opportune time to address performance issues and seek answers to your urgent questions, the key is *when* that should take place during the meeting. A former colleague, Kevin Gaither (a.k.a. the Godfather of Inside Sales), shared with me his one-on-one structure when I was a newbie manager, and I've lived by it ever since. The first half of the session is your report's time. This is their time to ask you questions, get advice, request approvals, etc. The second half is your time. Use this time wisely . . .

3. Clear Link Between Work and Company Objectives

When leading by faith, you learn to put your faith in your employees. This facilitates greater trust and transparency, allowing your reports to have that clear connection between their efforts and overall business objectives. When you micromanage—a key sign of a lack of trust—you remove the ability for employees to operate autonomously, and you eventually erode their drive to go above and beyond. Most employees who have a micromanager feel trapped and aren't willing to work as hard as they would if they had some autonomy. You are literally taking them out of the driver's seat of reaching the objectives you've laid out for them. Not trusting employees to do their job also shifts their focus from connecting their job to the overall business to thinking, *How do I keep my leader off my back?* This is not helpful. They eventually check out, which is disastrous for engagement, retention, and hitting business objectives.

As found in the research, helping employees see the connection between their work and overall company objectives—and not making them feel like an untrusted worker bee—is key to employee engagement and satisfaction. How can you participate in moving the business forward, consistently putting in more effort and more energy, if you don't understand that connection? It's damn near impossible.

4. Recognition

One of the most important lessons any leader can learn is to praise in public and discipline in private. The key is doing both. It is important to call out mistakes constructively. Unless you employ robots, humans are fallible and make mistakes. You're not doing your team any justice by avoiding conflict and *not* discussing errors or other areas of improvement. Do so constructively and with remedies to assist in their learning and improvement. It's equally important to recognize and reward their successes. Don't go overboard and start throwing out meaningless praises for day-to-day activities; save it for the examples. Give every employee a bar to aim for, but give both positive and negative, yet constructive, feedback so your employees trust your honesty and always know how they are performing.

5. Career Development

This is similar to the previous learning and development factor, but it's specific to *career* development, not just in their current role. This should really be called mentorship. This requires you to take time to discuss and provide guidance on future goals, which may or may not include moving the person out of your team or even organization. Selfishly, it can be difficult for leaders to even think about broaching the topic of moving an employee, especially a productive employee, out of their team or company.

Some of the best relationships I've built and greatest fulfillment I've personally had as a leader came from these career development conversations. Yes, I've guided many employees over the years into other roles, and some even into other companies. It's what was best for them and signified the attainment of a goal. During that process, how do you think they performed for me? At the absolute top of their game.

Gratitude does amazing things for employee engagement, morale, and productivity. Give it a try. You can start by simply asking your employees to outline their goals (personal and professional, to open this door) for the next six-to-twelve months. You'll find many people who have no idea where to go next, and you'll have an amazing opportunity to help them create those goals. You'll have others who have unrealistic goals, which is a great opportunity to offer support and a kind reality check. And you'll have a mix of folks who know exactly what they want. Most will be so amazed and appreciative that you asked. It's really a wonderful experience to be part of.

If one thing is clear today, it's that no two people are alike. That is *wonderful!* Don't get me started on all the proof that diversity—of thought, background, gender, ethnicity, sexual orientation, etc.— amplifies success significantly. Diversity in style of leadership can be beneficial too. As we get into the details of the following leadership styles, think about which traits you want to exhibit as a leader, what your inner leader looks like, and whether you are leading yourself and others with faith.

One of the most important traits to work on is your mindset. This goes for leaders, teachers, coaches, parents, students—literally everyone. But I can guarantee you will be a more successful leader with far more impact if you can develop and encourage a growth mindset.

My goal in the following chapter isn't to give a directive on which style of leadership should be embodied by all leaders. Each style has its merits and potential negatives, some more than others. There is room for integrating the most natural components of any or all of these styles to your life and the needs of your environment or team. A greater understanding of how to work within these styles and create your own authentic style that fits your purpose is key.

6

KNOWING YOUR STYLE

As you've probably gathered, I believe that every person has the ability to change a relationship for the better. That includes the leader and subordinate relationship. In my never-ending pursuit of leadership excellence, I have read quite a bit about leadership styles and compared them to my own experiences and observations. Regardless of whether you are a leader or employee, whether you like the leadership styles you deal with on a day-to-day basis or don't, you are not helpless.

The following leadership style descriptions—as researched in an article published by the *International Journal of Innovation and Technology Management*—are intended to help you identify what mix of styles you are dealing with and/or exhibit, the pros and cons of each, and some food for thought on the best ways to integrate and improve upon them.[1] We'll dig into some of the most commonly recognized styles of leadership, tips for leaders on potential areas for improvement, and tips for employees on how to make the most of each leadership style. I hope you take away some methods you can use to make the most of the different styles you are encountering and then use that knowledge to improve your daily life and propel you forward on your path to success.

AUTHORITATIVE LEADERSHIP

Focused on efficiency and results, this style typically includes a single point of power. Authoritarian leaders can be perceived as somewhat militant, making decisions alone or with a small group and expecting employees to fall in line without question. However, the most successful authoritarian leaders lead by example, inspiring employees to follow. They also set the vision for the organization or team, providing employees with clarity on how their role contributes to the long-term vision. This style is most effective with employees that need a lot of supervision or have little to no experience. With employees that are more experienced or those that aim to be on a high-growth trajectory, this style can stifle creativity and create frustration as there tends to be a "know your place, don't deviate" expectation of them.

This style of leadership may feel old-school and may also be referred to as autocratic. It is one of the oldest and most used leadership styles, even in today's world. Some authoritative leaders have found ways to take the best components of this style in combination with other styles to create something effective—primarily when they foster employee engagement, empowerment, and professional development, which are often lacking in the traditional authoritarian playbook.

Some pros of this style include clear vision, clear roles and structure, and letting employees see how their work ties into the long-term vision of the team or organization. Some cons include little room for creativity or innovation, too few seats at the table (i.e., lack of diversity of thought), and a lack of focus on employee development.

Let's look at a few examples of leaders who exhibit and succeed in authoritative leadership roles.

"People work better when they know what the goal is and why. It is important that people look forward to coming to work in the morning and enjoy working."
—ELON MUSK[2]

Elon Musk inspires his team with his ambitious, future-shaping visions. He sets stretch goals, and given the objectives, motivates and drives employees to go beyond their perceived limits. However, he has a tendency to be a bit of a micromanager, according to employees. While he's more than willing to put in one-hundred hours a week, his obsession with the details puts a lot of pressure on his employees, which can rub people the wrong way. Employees have been known to state that there is only one decision maker at Tesla—and it's Musk himself.

The authoritative style of leadership, particularly with the added component of micromanagement, isn't my favorite. However, when you hold yourself to the same (or higher) standard as your employees and genuinely seek to share a clear vision with direct correlation to the work of your employees as Musk's employees have reported, I'm inclined to say he's doing more than alright. Consider that as you evaluate your leadership style.

"To me, leadership is not about necessarily being the loudest in the room, but instead being a bridge, or the thing that is missing in the discussion and trying to build a consensus from there."

—JACINDA ARDERN[3]

Jacina Ardern is the youngest female prime minister of New Zealand, and it's great to see her leadership praised amid the COVID-19 pandemic. Ardern has managed to harness an authoritative leadership style in her efforts to make quick and impactful decisions while remaining kind, communicating clearly, and displaying empathy for her people. Her blend of quick, decisive action and genuine care for the people she serves is a refreshing take on this style of leadership, and one that I think all leaders can learn from. Generating a sense of relatability in office cannot be an easy task to achieve, but she's managed to do it and retain incredible approval ratings, which I attribute to her open and welcoming demeanor.

While these are excellent examples of leaders thriving in the authoritative style of leadership, there are pitfalls to every style of leadership. In authoritative leadership, many of the pitfalls are concerned with money. Hiring typically includes salary negotiations to save money, with no clear-cut salary bands. There's probably a discrepancy among salaries in the same role due to the negotiations, and since women are far less likely than men to negotiate, guess where those discrepancies likely lie? Pay can sometimes be lower than comparable companies as leaders are stuck in the past in terms of what is reasonable in the current market. Raises and promotions tend to be hard fought and not terribly exciting. Bonuses are often reserved for the highest echelon of roles, leaving the so-called worker bees feeling overworked and undervalued.

Another pitfall here is that employee retention hinges primarily on feelings of loyalty versus employee fulfillment and satisfaction, leaving a demoralized workforce.

If these components describe your own style of leadership, do not fear. There are ways to avoid these pitfalls.

1. **Start with a salary review of your employees after researching current market averages.** The days of salary secrecy are gone, so discrepancies won't be a secret for long. If you don't have salary bands and do allow negotiation on salary, you probably have a lower average salary for the women on your team than men. Correct that, making sure you factor in experience and tenure. Stick to those new bands or tiers for all new hires; you'll insulate yourself from lawsuits and avoid the biggest employee satisfaction pitfall there is: poor pay.

2. **Openly invite feedback.** Employees need to feel heard. If you don't often receive feedback, it may be because your team doesn't think it's welcome. Keep an open ear. You don't have to agree with or implement everything you hear, but it can help guide your decisions and will prevent your team from feeling unheard, which often leads to feeling unvalued.

3. **Encourage problem solving.** Lighten the load by encouraging employees to offer up solutions to problems, and truly consider them. If the solution doesn't work, explain why you feel that way and invite the person to revise their suggested solution or engage in a brainstorming session. This is a great

way to not only get them more involved and eventually solve problems before they reach you, but it's also a great lesson in what solutions you'll buy into, further buffering you from all of the day-to-day problems you may be drowning in currently.

4. **Broaden the power spectrum.** Give high performing members of your team the opportunity to take on more responsibility and make decisions. I call this Plate Pulling. In leadership, it can be overwhelming to have a constantly full plate with more and more being piled on. Let your team take things off your plate, which will save you time and help them to grow as well as feel more engaged. Work at delegating some of the decisions as you build trust with your team. Your calendar and your team will thank you for it.

If you lean toward this style of leadership and are prone to micromanaging, give yourself the Elon test. Are you doing work that has widespread impact? Are you Elon-level genius? Are you holding yourself to the same (or higher) standards as your employees? Are you fostering your employees' growth and inspiring them along the way? If not, dive into the other leadership styles, see where you can borrow traits, and tweak your style to ensure your team doesn't start to jump ship.

If these attributes describe your boss, there are several ways to manage up to this style of leader. First, communicate with respect. I know, I know, there can be so many feelings when you report to an authoritarian style—or old-school—leader. Few of them inspire respect, more often resentment, but sitting in your resentment isn't getting you anywhere, except maybe fired. . . . So consider trying something new. This type of leader will generally soften when shown respect. Aim for tact and respect in your communication to set the stage for a more fruitful conversation.

Second, consider What's in It for Me (WIIFM) or them. Most of the people under this style of leadership are longing for mentorship and guidance on how to grow and improve, as that's not often freely given under authoritative leadership. While I always recommend finding a mentor in your leader, you may want to consider managing up to this type of leader *and* seeking a willing mentor inside or outside of your organization. The trick to managing up is to seek out as much guidance as you can from this type of leader and clearly provide a WIIFM. Instead of demanding guidance from A to Z, focus on a specific goal or direction you want guidance on and tie it back to how it will help you perform your current role more effectively. If at all possible, tie it back to revenue.

Finally, be consistent. You are likely to get the brush off from this type of leader, so you're going to need to take initiative in scheduling time to get the support and guidance you need, and you're going to need to follow up to ensure the guidance keeps coming. Is it fair? No. In an ideal world, your boss would be just as invested in your growth as you are. But when that's not the case, you've got to take matters into your own hands. Many leaders will learn and adapt quickly to this previously unacknowledged need, but those that refuse to change or offer support are the type that make you really consider whether that role/team/company is the right fit for you. And guess what? It's okay if it's not. We're talking about a job, not a marriage. It is not "'til death do you part."

Lessons from this style that can help you on your path to success, whether the goal is professional or not:

◊ **Are you inviting feedback?** If you aren't sure, simply consider how frequently you receive feedback from those involved in your goal (and that includes your support system). If the answer is rarely or never, you are likely not giving off vibes of being open to feedback, so you'll have to ask for it directly to get the ball rolling. From there, monitor your response to feedback so you don't inadvertently communicate that you don't actually want to receive it.

◊ **Are you encouraging collaboration?** Similar to the above, if you aren't noticing others jumping in to collaborate, you may not be communicating that it's welcome. Ask whether others feel collaboration is encouraged, and what they need from you to facilitate it. The answer could simply be an open call to ideas and participation in projects until it becomes second nature to all involved to raise their hands.

◊ **Are you holding yourself to the same high standards you have of others involved?** One of the best ways to gain respect as a leader and inspire those around you to give their all is to hold yourself to the same expectations, if not higher, than those around you. Being the leader in your big, hairy, audacious goal is no different. If you can demonstrate to those around you that you are in the trenches with them and not shouting orders from the sidelines, you'll be amazed at how much more respect you'll receive and how much more you all will accomplish together.

◊ **Are you clear on vision and how their support/efforts tie into the end goal?** The idea here is not to shout meaningless orders from the sidelines for the sake of shouting orders. Providing clear insight into how each and every person involved in accomplishing your goal factors into the vision you have will fortify their motivation when the going gets tough.

◊ **Are you giving people room to learn and grow through the process, or micromanaging every step of the way?** If you're not sure, ask. If you think you're sure, ask anyway. If you know you tend to micromanage, ask yourself why . . . and ask them if that's working.

DIRECTIVE LEADERSHIP

Leaders employing a directive style operate from a pyramid-like structure where power, instruction, and communication moves top-down. Unlike the authoritarian style, the power dynamic under directive leadership is more distributed layer-by-layer; so while there is a clear structure, there are more seats at the table within the team or organization. Unfortunately, this style still doesn't allow for a tremendous amount of collaboration or innovation, as there tends to be coercion using rewards and punishments to control the direction of employees. Rewards and punishment aren't inherently negative, though the perceived threat of punishment for stepping outside of one's box or failing leads people to being less willing to take risks or offer up ideas.

That said, this style does provide consistency. Typically, each level of employee or leader understands expectations and the rewards or punishments for their performance. It does produce predictable employee performance but at the sacrifice of flexibility and innovation.

Some pros of this style include clarity of role and behavioral expectations, consistency, and a rinse-and-repeat method. Cons are that directive leadership is inflexible, there's little to no room for collaboration or innovation, and there is a possible absence of individual mentorship and guidance.

> *"If it is not possible for me to go somewhere and to be willing to encounter people with different views, then I'm really not doing my job."*
>
> —CONDOLEEZZA RICE[4]

As the first female African American secretary of state in the United States and highest-ranking African American female in US history (until Kamala Harris became vice president in 2021), Condoleezza Rice is a directive leader whom I feel compelled to share. Her ability to adjust her leadership style to the needs of each project or situation that came her way should be praised. Her natural style has elements of directive leadership, which is why I mention her here. I have to commend her ability to tailor her style to the task at hand, something I wish more leaders would exemplify. One of the best examples of her directive leadership was her strong and clear communication skills, ensuring all of her team members were clear on what needed to be done in times such as the aftermath of the September 11 attacks on the World Trade Center: leveraging the skills of each member on her team, but ultimately ensuring she was the final decision maker to keep progress moving in the right direction. As you can see by her quote, Condoleezza Rice did not fall into the authoritarian-esque, directive-leadership trap of being the only mind that mattered, but rather sought to use all resources available to make the best decisions for her team and for everyone relying on her. Her openness to other ideas and values makes her an exemplary directive leader.

"The only place success comes before work is in the dictionary."

—VINCE LOMBARDI[5]

I include Vince Lombardi here not because he led my favorite team, the Green Bay Packers, to five National Football League championships—including Super Bowls I and II—but because his flavor of leadership may have been classified as directive. It was quite inspirational and pushed every player and coach who worked alongside him to constantly reach for their potential, fostering a growth mindset among them all. Lombardi held his team accountable to incredibly high standards and wasn't afraid to part with players who weren't willing to put in the work. What made him so effective was that he equally held himself accountable. The directive leadership style can quickly have you falling on your face or looking like a jerk if you don't lead by example. Employees are far more inclined to go above and beyond for someone they know is in it *with* them and not just benefiting *from* them.

There are other pitfalls as well that I've seen this leadership style result in, which may aid in identifying this style in yourself or your boss. These include the potential for creating authoritarians in each subsequent layer, micromanagement, leaders being less responsive to feedback, and less employee satisfaction if role guidelines are too rigid, making their ability to create impact feel stifled.

If components of this style describe you, here are some tips to avoid pitfalls associated with this style in order to create a more satisfactory and supportive environment for your employees:

1. **Poll your team.** You don't have to buy any crazy software to pull off an anonymous survey that allows your employees to provide feedback on what is great and not so great in their current environment. Be prepared for the responses to sting a

bit, but know that nearly all of these surveys will come back showing a need for improvement in communication.

2. **Focus on employee development.** You'll likely find that your employees want more one-on-one time with you or their direct manager in the survey above. The simplest way to meet the needs of your employees is to meet regularly one-on-one. The first one-on-one should set the stage by explaining how the meetings will flow and discussing the employee's goals—personal and professional—over the next six-to-twelve months. It's important to open the door to the personal in these meetings. Understanding the whole person is key to helping them grow, adding value to their experience, and gives you greater insight into how best to guide them.

3. **Lead by example.** Regardless of whether you sit at the top of the hierarchy, be careful to avoid the pitfalls explained above, and encourage other leaders within your sphere of influence to do the same. If you can harness the clarity of vision that this style promotes coupled with emotional intelligence in the people-management aspects, you'll find yourself with a more communicative, committed, and engaged team of employees.

This leadership style may feel necessary in organizations with large headcounts, departments, or teams. That said, I'd highly recommend finding a bridge between clear guidelines, consistent performance, taking advantage of motivational tools, having clear policies that outline consequences, and encouraging the spirit of innovation, creativity, and collaboration. Finding the right mix can create inspiring directive leaders who create the necessary clarity and vision to get teams to push beyond existing performance standards.

If these attributes describe your boss, you should think before you speak. Leaders that operate under a directive style tend to be hyperfocused on details and clarity, so it's important that you avoid bringing up half-baked ideas or thoughts that haven't been thought through enough to withstand the follow-up questions that will more than likely be asked. Take the time to anticipate the questions your boss will have about an idea, suggestion, or change, and be prepared. It never hurts to get another teammate's opinion and work through some of the details together before presenting to your boss.

You can also offer assistance. There is less of a power grab under directive leadership than authoritarian, so you just might find growth opportunities for yourself if you simply offer to help. I often think of leadership as somewhat of a circus act, balancing multiple spinning plates while new plates come flying into the mix constantly. People who offer to handle one or more of those plates are often seen as a godsend to leaders, and handling that additional responsibility can lead to more opportunities. I speak from personal experience when I say it can be difficult to keep your eyes on all the spinning plates and identify how to distribute them, so offer up your help if you want to get your hands on to something new. It could just be the wake-up call your leader needs to realize they don't have to do it all by themselves.

Lastly, take charge of your experience. Does this mean just do whatever you feel like? No. I'm not trying to get anyone fired here; please don't do that. What it does mean is if you feel like you need additional training or education to further contribute to the team or organization and to aid in your personal development, bring the need(s) to your leader. If you can see room to take on more responsibility that would allow you to contribute more and allow your leader to feel less like a circus act, speak up. If you're told no, ask to understand why. But don't give up. Learn what parameters they use for making their decisions, and try to speak to those parameters when bringing ideas to the table.

This style of leadership lends itself well to large team structures that need a lather-rinse-and-repeat component to them. As someone who thrives on seeing potential in people, fostering that potential, and witnessing the power of individual growth in those around them, I find this style of leadership necessary in small doses but often too rigid. Granted, I've primarily worked at tech startups where I've built teams from scratch and needed to foster employee growth to keep up with the pace of the organization's expansion.

In my opinion, those leveraging a directive leadership style should use it in small doses, if only to clarify roles and create consistency for large teams, but side-by-side with a more growth-oriented people management style to prevent them from running their team into the ground and/or creating an environment where top talent winds up leaving due to a potential lack of growth opportunities.

Lessons from this style that can help you on your path to success, whether the goal is professional or not:

◊ **Have you made their role and your expectations clear?** It's imperative to have an open dialogue about what you need and expect so that everyone is clear, and to know if you are going to get the support you need or if you need to find others to fill the holes.

◊ **Are you holding yourself equally accountable to your role?**

◊ **Are there elements of progress that you can design to be lather-rinse-and-repeat?**

◊ **Are you giving away too much power or expecting others to do all the work?** Make sure you're in the driver's seat if this is your goal. Now, if you're reading this as you are pursuing a goal with others, be sure to share the helm, leveraging each person's strengths that are involved. The more everyone is involved and committed when all benefit from reaching success, the more empowered and connected to getting there they'll be.

◊ **Are you allowing collaboration?** Diversity of thought and true open dialogue is the best way to generate better and better ideas. If you have others supporting you, ensure you open the door to collaboration and innovation in the name of working smarter, not harder.

PARTICIPATIVE LEADERSHIP

The participative, or democratic, leadership style includes the employees in decision-making. So much about what motivates us as humans and employees has been studied, but what has contributed considerably to the growth in this style of leadership is Abraham Maslow's "A Theory of Human Motivation," in which he outlines the most basic needs that have to be met to motivate us humans.[6] Maslow's hierarchy of needs helps to explain the approach taken in a participative leadership style: belonging. Studies have shown that employees are both more productive and more satisfied when they are recognized and participate in activities. When the most basic needs of food, safety, love, belonging, and esteem are met, humans are more motivated to grow and achieve goals.

So it makes sense that many modern companies are moving away from a hierarchy of power and to flatter organizations that include and empower employees. Arranging employees and management in this way naturally fosters participation. The more involved an employee is in a decision, change, or vision, the more motivated they will be to see it through to completion.

Some pros of this style include engaged employees, seeking diversity of thought to generate better ideas and decisions, and fostering a sense of belonging and ability to impact. Cons could be leaning too far toward collective decision-making, slowing things down or preventing decisions from being made, and over-communicating issues that may not be productive or necessary for employees to know.

"Most companies target women as end users, but few are effectively utilizing female employees when it comes to innovating for female consumers. When women are empowered in the design and innovation process, the likelihood of success in the marketplace improves by 144 percent!"

—INDRA NOOYI[7]

As a successful businesswoman and president and CEO of Pepsi-Co Inc. from 2006 to 2017 who led several acquisitions leading to a $22 billion valuation,[7] Indra Nooyi is certainly an inspiration. More impressive was her style of leading through inclusion, appreciation of the skills and talents amongst her employees, and ability to make great decisions that guided the company's success to new heights.

"Concepts are more reality based, because it costs so much money to develop them . . . We use them as a learning tool. We'd sorely miss the opportunity if we didn't listen to people."

—JIM LENTZ[8]

Jim Lentz is the former CEO of Toyota, and while this quote is more reflective of the importance Lentz placed on listening to customers, it is demonstrative of his understanding that participation and a listening ear provides learning opportunities that foster growth. Being transparent about the value of hearing both customers and employees is a great way to encourage participative leadership and generates a greater likelihood of garnering impactful feedback. This style of leadership can easily be undermined if the goal isn't clearly communicated. Imagine a leader who doesn't verbalize the reason why they accept and act on feedback; you might be inclined to think they simply can't make decisions or are riding on the coattails of their team. But a leader who is clear about the value they place on hearing their team and customers will naturally gain respect and foster a greater sense of belonging within their team.

Some pitfalls I've seen this leadership style result in, which may aid in identifying this style in yourself or your boss, include half effort and too much transparency. Most people are drawn to the benefits of the participative style of leadership, but actually embracing the act of encouraging and fostering participation takes more effort than you might think. Half efforts can cause more harm than good, e.g., communicating the desire to include employees in decision-making but not actually doing it will foster twice as much resentment as simply not giving them a voice. Additionally, when attempting to include employees in decisions, leaders can swing too far in the attempt at transparency, creating a sea of panic if issues or disagreements that don't affect them are too openly shared. Let's face it, most organizations have some amount of internal drama and sharing every bit of it with your employees when it doesn't affect them or when you are resolving it before it reaches them simply does more harm than good.

If components of this style describe you, in order to create a more satisfactory and supportive environment for your employees, you should:

1. **Communicate your goal.** When employing a participative leadership style, it's imperative that you clearly communicate why you are encouraging such open participation and idea sharing from your team. A lot of people have leadership PTSD from past experiences where their boss asked for their ideas and then took credit for it. Be clear that your goal is to encourage diversity of thought and commit to giving credit where credit is due.

2. **Act on your goal.** When members of your team share their feedback and ideas with you, be sure to listen to understand and sincerely consider the feedback and ideas. It's impossible for 100 percent of the participation to be correct or easy to implement. It's important for you to first seek to understand and then involve them in the process of fine-tuning or adjusting the subsequent actions required; otherwise, you'll turn those team members off from continuing to be so open with you.

3. **Set clear expectations.** If you have a large team or a more communicative team in general, you may feel overwhelmed by the amount of feedback or ideas you receive. Be clear that the goal is not for you to become the complaint department. Instead, they should primarily come to you with a problem or concern, as well as at least one to two possible solutions. Putting the problem solving in their hands will keep you from feeling overwhelmed with a seemingly endless pile of issues and will empower them to put their problem-solver hat on.

If this describes your boss, you should give feedback! Don't sit back silently, but share your ideas, suggestions, solutions, and feedback on things that can be improved.

Keep communicating. Let's face it, no boss is perfect and there will be times when you may feel like your ideas and feedback aren't really listened to. Be open about those times and listen to understand how your boss best receives feedback. Be careful not to simply bring them problems; instead come forward with possible solutions. This will help them see your desire to fix whatever issues you present. It's also important that you become or continue to be an active participant in your own growth path. If they don't know what gives you the most fulfillment, they can't ensure you have the opportunity to tap into it.

Lastly, open the door for feedback. In this style of leadership, it can feel like the feedback door only swings one way: to them. But it's important that you follow suit and communicate your desire to receive feedback. Knowing where you can improve, what you're doing well, etc., will only help you on your path to success.

Lessons from this style that can help you on your path to success, whether the goal is professional or not:

◊ **Communication is key.** Any member of your team or support system should clearly understand your desire for feedback and ideas. Remember, diversity of thought is crucial to finding the best solutions and steps to take regardless of the goal you seek to achieve.

◊ **Keep an open mind.** It's easy to become slightly (or for many of us, extremely) stubborn when you're charging toward a goal that is personal to you. Being open to others' experiences and expertise can only help you. This doesn't mean you should do everything someone else says or what's worked for them, but keeping an open mind will give you more options to consider as you carve out the optimal path toward success.

◊ **Ask yourself these questions:**
  › Am I enlisting the help and feedback of others when it comes to this goal?
  › Have I communicated my openness to feedback and suggestions?
  › Are there people in my support system who can lend some advice that might give me an upper hand on this path?

SERVANT LEADERSHIP

I'm just going to say it: servant leadership is at the top of my list in terms of favorite leadership styles, largely because it works incredibly well not only for fostering growth and developing leadership across the organization, but also because it typically seeks input from customer-facing employees. Having spent the majority of my career managing customer-facing roles, it's something I value tremendously and have witnessed the power of doing.

When you think of servant leadership, the words "inclusion" and "synergy" should come to mind. This style of leadership is another that operates in a decentralized organizational structure, with the goal of setting a vision and strategy. However, the implementation is done by offering support to employees, encouraging innovation, engagement, and the development of leadership qualities among employees. Learning how to lead isn't just for "leaders." Employees who learn how to lead are able to grow more personally and in all aspects of work.

Pros of servant leadership include improved retention of customers by enlisting the help of customer-facing employees to provide input on products and solutions, increased employee engagement (remember Maslow's hierarchy of needs—feeling seen, heard, and understood is the key to keeping employees engaged), and employee development—thus more opportunities for growth. Some cons include, as with participative leadership, that this style can go wrong if the leader fails to assert some level of authority. Without empathy, great listening skills, or commitment to developing employees, this style can quickly feel like an empty gesture and squash all the pros listed above. It's important to keep in mind that servant leadership is not suitable for all leaders (e.g., military leaders must typically assume complete authority).

"There is one red line that we should not cross. It is a commitment to human rights, the respect of the dignity of the human being. There should be no compromises."

—ANGELA MERKEL[9]

Immediately upon becoming chancellor of Germany in 2005, Angela Merkel established her style of leadership in office: one of a servant leader. Throughout her time in office, Merkel sought to serve the people of Germany as well as all humans in need. While her openness to refugees wasn't always met with excitement or approval, it demonstrates her vision as a servant to humankind. One of her best traits is the ability to pause and look objectively at a situation before finding a solution while keeping the people involved in mind—something all leaders should strive to exhibit.

"A leader . . . is like a shepherd. He stays behind the flock, letting the most nimble go out ahead, whereupon the others follow, not realizing that all along they are being directed from behind."

—NELSON MANDELA[10]

There is no question about the commitment Nelson Mandela had to serving the greater good. In fact, he was jailed for twenty-seven years for his efforts and beliefs about equality. Many people would be driven to give up their mission after such a lengthy sentence and the abuse he endured throughout his incarceration, but Mandela persevered and eventually became the first president of South Africa from 1994–1999. His government's primary focus was on dismantling apartheid and generating equality for all, resulting in the creation of a multiracial government. His ability to fight such a difficult battle while maintaining an attitude of forgiveness and selflessness is to be admired and, hopefully, replicated by as many leaders as possible.

Let's look at some of the pitfalls servant leadership can result in. Listening to respond versus listening to understand is one pitfall I've seen this leadership style result in. This can cause employees to feel as though no listening was done at all. It's important to check your ego at the door when attempting to embody the servant leadership style, meaning your goal is not to immediately respond or negate feedback or ideas given by team members, but rather to hear them out and follow up with questions to aid in your understanding. Active listening is imperative to successfully pulling off this style of leadership . . . or really any leadership style.

Another potential pitfall is a servant leader becoming a doormat. While most people who identify as a servant leader tend to be people pleasers, they must maintain some level of authority, or they may find themselves implementing every idea or making every requested change—regardless of how well those ideas or changes solve the problems intended or whether they are things that can be maintained or scaled as the business grows.

Demonstrating empathy and commitment to the development of employees is critical in this, and in truly all, styles of leadership. Without those two characteristics, leaders may find themselves frustrated with the pace at which some employees learn and be tempted to give up. It's important to remember that everyone learns at a different pace and has different obstacles to overcome in their development. Without this understanding, the power of developing employees can be lost or severely diminished.

To avoid pitfalls associated with this style:

1. **First show empathy.** While opening the door to feedback can be intimidating or create frustrations over the seemingly useless feedback that can and will, from time to time, come your way, it's important to show empathy to your team. There will be people who are being asked for feedback for the first time in their career who may open the floodgates and still need time to learn how to filter or spend more time analyzing a situation before presenting it and their idea or solution to you. Be slow-tempered, even when you've had a long, stressful day, and compassionately communicate clearer expectations about how to best present ideas or solutions to you.

2. **Be a servant, not a slave.** Remember that you are attempting to embody servant leadership, not indentured servitude. As with parenting, part of serving those under your leadership is to help them to grow, even if it means delivering constructive criticism and discipline. So long as the end goal

is to help them grow versus jump at their every whim, you are toeing the line well.

3. **Stay committed.** Some seeds take root and bloom faster than others; the same will be true with your team. If you can focus on being committed to each member's unique path and growth needs, you'll find fulfillment in their development. Employee development isn't a one-size-fits-all solution, so don't lose hope when you've got a combination of hyper-growth and slower-growth people on your team. Some will grow more than others, some have more desire to grow and develop than others, but so long as you stay committed, you can be confident that you are embracing servant leadership and offering your support for their specific needs.

If this describes your boss, you should ask for guidance. You're going to get a lot more out of a servant leader if you speak up than if you attempt to go it alone or expect them to telepathically understand what you need. Not all leaders are so inclined to support and help you develop, so take advantage of the privilege you have to work with a leader who finds value in your growth. If you're uncertain of what your next goal should be, have an open conversation with them about where they think you can grow and what steps it will take to get there. Great leaders will often see your potential before you even recognize it, so ask for help and guidance on how to maximize that potential.

As an employee under this leadership style, you should also be communicative. Openly share your feedback and solutions to issues you or your customers are facing. Do the work of attempting to find possible solutions versus simply bringing issues to your boss, but if you can't find a solution, don't withhold the information. Instead, present the issue at hand and let them know you haven't been able to find a solution. This will leverage their desire to support and guide without letting issues go unseen.

Lessons from this style that can help you on your path to success, whether the goal is professional or not:

◊ **How are you serving others with what you aim to accomplish?** There is great fulfillment in helping others, so if you can identify ways in which achieving your goal will be of use to others, you'll tap into yet another motivation that will keep you focused and disciplined on your path.

◊ **Ask for help!** Servant leadership teaches us that asking for help and serving others aren't separate things—they often work in tandem. As you can see from this style of leadership, they help others to grow by serving them and asking them to help come up with solutions, ideas, etc. If you can manage to seek help on your journey to success, you will likely find that it helps others see what they are most skilled at and find fulfillment in supporting you. Don't let your ego prevent you from asking for help or guidance. That will only slow you down.

◊ **Commitment is crucial.** As I've explained, servant leaders have to remember that not every person grows at the same speed, and so many factors contribute to that: major life events, personal awareness, etc. The same is true as you march down the path to success. There will be times where it feels like a sprint; others where you feel as if you're trudging through quicksand. Stay the course, remain committed, and you will find success at the end of that road.

TRANSFORMATIONAL LEADERSHIP

Successful organizations around the globe are constantly changing and evolving—transforming, if you will. Transformational leaders recognize this, and harness the power of employee job satisfaction and engagement to keep disrupting and innovating. This style of leadership is aimed primarily at inspiring and empowering employees to make changes that benefit them and their customers. Transformational leaders serve as the example for employees to model themselves after, constantly innovating and being involved in organizational culture and structural changes to facilitate constant growth both personally and for the organization. In this leadership style, there is more power given to the employee to decide what their focus should be and what they need to execute on, generally with no set rules or expectations, to enable their creativity and innovation to bear fruit.

Transformational leadership creates an atmosphere of trust, gives generation and communication of new ideas, and provides opportunity for creativity and innovation. Some cons include the risk of employees not following through, not being a great fit for employees who need guidance and supervision (i.e., rules and expectations), and the fact that this style doesn't work very well in bureaucratic structures where clearer rules and expectations are needed.

"The size of your dreams must always exceed your current capacity to achieve them.
If your dreams do not scare you, they are not big enough."
—ELLEN JOHNSON SIRLEAF[11]

Talk about a woman with a mission! Ellen Johnson Sirleaf was the first democratically-elected female head of state in Africa and served as president of Liberia from 2006 to 2018. Throughout her presidency and political career, she sought and achieved positive economic, social, and political change. Sirleaf is internationally recognized as a leader in women's empowerment. She was awarded the Nobel Peace Prize in 2011, and also received the Presidential Medal of Freedom for her commitment to freedom and improving the lives of Africans. Sirleaf spent her time tackling some of the biggest dreams one can imagine, inspiring others to follow her lead, and leaving lasting change in her wake.

"I believe the choice to be excellent begins with aligning your thoughts
and words with the intention to require more from yourself."
—OPRAH WINFREY[12]

I can't share examples of transformational leaders without mentioning Oprah Winfrey. Imagine sitting in a conference room and hearing that quote from Oprah herself. Talk about inspiring. There is no doubt about the values that Oprah holds and the inspiration she brings to all around her, including viewers and fans. Her message has always clearly been one of personal growth, a high moral and ethical standard, and finding purpose. A great transformational leader will leave you feeling inspired and motivated regardless of the amount of work to be done.

Still, there are some pitfalls to transformational leadership. Using this style of leadership with less creative employees or roles can be disastrous. It's almost a sink-or-swim mentality that doesn't bode well for people newer to the workforce or those needing clear-cut rules and expectations in order to be successful in their role. Also, while it may seem laissez-faire in approach, it's important to keep up to date on employee progress to ensure they aren't drowning in the open waters of autonomy and to offer guidance when people are struggling.

If components of this style describe you, to avoid pitfalls, you should:

1. **Keep communication open.** Some employees will flourish under this style of leadership, and others will struggle. Remember that one of the key components of a successful transformational leader is to provide mentoring and coaching. Keep pushing the employees who naturally succeed in this environment and make sure you are checking in with and guiding those who struggle. A lot of people get blinded by fear when they are given autonomy and can't see how to accomplish what they need or want to; be the lantern that helps light their way.

2. **Never stop looking for ways to motivate.** Again, some people will take off under transformational leadership, and others will be paralyzed by doubt and fear at the starting line. Your job is to continuously look for ways to inspire and motivate all your employees, regardless of how naturally they thrive under this style of leadership. Even though this style doesn't generally offer set rules and expectations, if you have an employee that needs clarity, offer them some general expectations and guide them toward creating their own once they've gotten the hang of it.

If this describes your boss, you should first be honest. If you find yourself feeling lost under this style of leadership, speak up. Your leader should be more than willing to offer mentoring and coaching to help you find your footing. The goal of this style is to foster both yours and the company's growth, so don't suffer in silence—ever. You should also share your ideas. Some leaders using this approach will simply expect you to voice your opinions and ideas, so whether you are directly asked for them or not, share them. The purpose of transformational leadership is to leverage every mind involved to innovate and create impactful change. Your ideas shouldn't go unnoticed.

Lessons from this style that can help you on your path to success, whether the goal is professional or not:

◊ **Are you seeking success or meaning on your journey toward your goal?** If you focus on meaning and purpose, your success will often be far greater than simply thinking of the achievement.

◊ **Does your work inspire and motivate others?** You'll have a far greater impact if it does. How can you use your goal to create a ripple effect of inspiration?

◊ **Are you leveraging all the minds you have access to in order to develop creative and innovative solutions or paths?**

SUMMARY: FOCUS ON YOUR TRAITS

You might have formed opinions on some of the styles we've discussed as "good" or "bad." Maybe you've experienced a manager with many poor traits who displayed one of the more direct or autocratic styles, and you are instantly reminded of all they did wrong and all the stress or lack of job satisfaction their traits and style brought you. You are not alone. I'll caution you, however, not to completely rule out any leadership style but to instead focus on the traits you want to exhibit as a leader. Always hold true to the traits you value. These may be compassion, ethics, or development; then test out the various leadership and communication styles that best fit the situation you are in. Again, note that you can integrate components of different styles into your life and leadership. Make it your own authentic style so you can thrive as you lead yourself and others.

It's not uncommon to have a negative reaction to the more directive or autocratic styles of leadership. However, there is a time and a place for everything. If you're a visionary like Elon Musk, I'm going to go ahead and say it's perfectly acceptable to be the primary person steering the ship. Does that mean you shouldn't value and trust your employees? Absolutely not! That's where developing your ideal leadership traits, like a growth mindset, comes in.

Trust me when I say I am not at all suggesting that a single leadership style is best. There's a time and a place for various styles of leadership, and there's also always room for continuous improvement for all leaders.

As we've explored each of these leadership styles, I hope you've taken away the importance of open communication and leading by faith. When I say open communication, I 100 percent mean one-on-ones in the work setting, but more specifically being direct in your communication. If there's an issue, a worry, a concern, it needs to be brought to light with an open mind and with the goal of resolving said issue, worry, or concern. Let's face it, some people are better at picking up signals than others. If all you do is give signals and expect everyone you interact with to understand what you're trying to say, you're creating an uneven playing field and setting others up for failure. Despite how uncomfortable it can feel to address things, especially when they lean more toward being negative than positive, it's important to communicate directly.

Leading by faith can mean many things. The Bible can speak to not only how we conduct ourselves but also how we treat those under our leadership. I liken a great leader to the Lord in Jeremiah 29:11, but who better to set as an example than God? This verse holds a special place in my heart and has truly guided my life, my career, and how I conduct myself.

"For I know the plans I have for you," declares the Lord, "plans to prosper you and not to harm you, plans to give you hope and a future."

—JEREMIAH 29:11(NIV)[13]

You see, God has always made Himself known in my life when I needed Him the most. He has always provided. My biggest prayer is to be used as His vessel, and I find it my responsibility to leave those under my leadership with that same feeling of comfort and caring as that verse gives me. All the plans I have are for my employees' good, whether it be a change in process, a training—or retraining—session, discipline, etc. I aim to teach, and I aim to help them improve now and in the future.

A former colleague had a great saying that I don't mind saying I copied because it's so great: "If you ever leave this team, it better be for something that moves you up to the next level of your career." This wasn't a threat; it was a promise. My job, as I see it, is to mold anyone under my leadership into the next best version of themselves and to help them get to the next level. Hopefully that's with me or with our company, but if not, I will always be happy for them so long as they move on for the next right thing. For their good. For a hope and a future.

The burden of leadership is large, but that also means the impact you can have is incredibly great. If you take that responsibility seriously and look for the ways to create a positive ripple as a result of your leadership—at work, at home, anywhere—you'll tap into fulfillment that extends far beyond yourself.

7

BEING PATIENT

Do you remember the patience song you heard as a child?

Have patience, have patience,
Don't be in such a hurry.
When you get impatient, you only start to worry.
Remember, remember, that God is patient too,
And think of all the times when others have to wait for you.

When you're focused on a goal, you've been charging down the path to reach it and the last thing you want to do is slow down. You want to sprint, hurdle, fly toward the finish line. Often, drive and motivation translate to this need for speed when it comes to achieving our goals. But patience is key. As the children's song above reminds us, when you get impatient, you only start to worry. How true is that?!

Much like fear, impatience can be a deterrent to success. It can actually cause you to avoid important tasks, lash out at those around you, and not get the rest you need to be fully focused. Prior to discovering the mindset hack I shared in chapter 1 (flipping frustrating situations to a focus on an inevitable positive or blessing), I often found myself being impatient. I probably wouldn't have called it that then because I felt it was a justifiable reaction to my situation.

At the time, I was frequently made promises that rarely came to fruition—from career opportunities to necessary business changes that would allow me to grow the business and earn a better income. Looking back, I can see that my impatience only achieved one thing: keeping me focused on what was not working. It derailed my solutions-oriented mind from looking for a way to improve my situation. It caused me to stress . . . and I stressed some more. It even bled into my personal life, creating tension at home unnecessarily.

Rather than do what I typically do best—set a goal, go after it, and achieve it—I couldn't seem to get out of my impatience loop. It took someone seeking me out as an ideal job candidate for me to realize what my goals were: to grow professionally, make more money, feel challenged, and make a real impact at work . . . and also not to be a Debbie Downer at home. Living impatiently is as productive for your success journey as literally walking in place. You don't get anywhere—except to further levels of impatience, frustration, and possibly even anger.

Can you think of a single example of a time when impatience made your life easier? Now how about patience and a calm demeanor? I thought so. Score for patience! As you progress toward your goals, you are going to need to fight impatience and fear, possibly simultaneously. But if you fortify your defenses with the knowledge that patience is a helpful tool in your quest, you'll come out ahead.

PATIENCE AND SELF-CONTROL

Let's dive into how impatience affects us . . .

Figure 7.1. Image shows man tapping fingers against a desk in an impatient manner.

Take a long, hard look at the previous image. The man pictured is clearly expressing impatience, but doesn't he also look angry? That's because those two emotions tend to be besties and like to work together—and not for your good. If you were sitting across from the man pictured, how likely would you be to listen to him or willingly follow his instructions or requests? In general, people find this kind of expression and demeanor anything but inspiring and are less likely to navigate toward cooperation. Worse, studies have shown the negative effect impatience (and anger) have on decision making and self-control.

One such study is the famous Marshmallow Test run by Walter Mischel, who was the Robert Johnston Niven professor of humane letters in the department of psychology at Columbia University. The basics of the study included offering preschoolers one marshmallow (or other treat) now or giving them two if they could wait (with the treat in front of them) for twenty minutes. In follow-up studies, the preschoolers who were able to wait achieved more success financially, academically, and professionally.[1] While the correlation between those who could wait and their future success has been somewhat controversial, as scientists have learned that self-control *can* be learned, it does highlight the importance of self-control when it comes to success. So, whether you were taught self-control as a child or not, you can develop it, and having the ability to wait will have a very real impact on your likelihood of success.

In 2002, Angela L. Duckworth and Martin E. P. Seligman discovered that self-control actually beats talent when predicting academic success in adolescence. In the years since, more and more evidence has surfaced showing that self-control helps with tackling day-to-day goals, especially when achieving those goals is interrupted by temptations that would halt progress or completion. Part of their drive to study the impact of self-control stemmed from Duckworth and Seligman witnessing students with plenty of learning aptitude and intellect fail in the classroom. They joined forces to identify the power of self-control, what it could predict, and whether it could be altered.

Their hypothesis was that, "The capacity to regulate attention, emotion, and behavior in the presence of temptation predicts academic success better than general intelligence."[2]

To test this hypothesis, they conducted a prospective, longitudinal study of local middle-school students. It started with a standardized IQ test, questionnaires about self-control—which were completed by the students, their parents, and their homeroom teachers—and delay-of-gratification tasks to round out the assessment of each student's self-control. At the end of the school year (seven months later), they reviewed official school records on each student's academic performance.

What they found was that while higher IQ scores did predict higher report card grades, the same was also true for the self-control measurement. In fact, the students who had made gains on their self-control rank showed higher report card grades, whereas the same was not true for IQ scores. After studying the psychology of achievement for years, Duckworth developed the following equation for achievement:

TALENT x EFFORT = SKILL

SKILL x EFFORT = ACHIEVEMENT

Figure 7.2. Equation for Achievement

In short, Duckworth defines talent as the speed at which you improve skill when you apply effort, and achievement is the result of using those acquired skills. While she explains in her book *Grit: The Power of Passion and Perseverance* that there are other factors at play when it comes to achievement—namely opportunities or having an excellent teacher, mentor, or coach—her theory is incredibly useful for our purposes. The fact that effort factors into achievement twice whereas talent only factors in once should leave you breathing a little easier. Not only does effort build skill, she says, but it also makes that skill productive.[3]

Will Smith is a great example of her theory, as noted in *Grit*. When explaining his success, Will Smith said, "I've never really viewed myself as particularly talented. Where I excel is ridiculous, sickening work ethic." The Fresh Prince himself acknowledges that his determination to never be outworked (effort) has led to the tremendous successes he's had in his life and career.[4]

I feel inclined to reference the slap heard around the world briefly. While I certainly don't condone physical violence as Smith unfortunately displayed at the Oscars in 2022, I do think it's a great opportunity to acknowledge that even those in the public eye are still human and make mistakes. Smith is a man with an incredible work ethic and generally demonstrates patience. But he's human. Without reviving the seemingly endless slap memes, I believe his mistake can serve as a lesson. You are human. You will make mistakes. From time to time, you will let negative emotions take over and you may regret your actions. Just as Smith issued a heartfelt apology and stated his commitment to doing better,[5] so can we. Don't give up on your journey to self-improvement after making a mistake, no matter how big or small it may be. Take accountability, refocus, and commit to doing better.

The point here is that your will (not Smith, but willpower), determination, effort, and self-control are absolutely indicative of your likelihood to succeed. Impatience is more akin to impulsivity than effort, and if you recall from chapter 4, impulsivity and delay will only dampen your motivation and slow your progress.

Does this mean we should condemn ourselves when impatience comes rushing in? I think you know me enough by now to say, "Of course not." However, tapping back into our Emotional Intelligence (EQ), we should absolutely put in the work to be more aware of when impatience is rising, identify the triggers that lead to those feelings, and find tools to stop it in its tracks before our progress stalls or goes off the rails.

PREVAILING THROUGH IMPATIENCE

We live in a world of on-demand everything, and it's trained most of us to crave instant gratification. When was the last time you rage clicked on a website that was loading too slowly or just said, "Forget it," and abandoned your session because who wants to sit and wait for a website to load? Impatience traps surround us, but we can prevail. When it comes to achieving your goal, you are likely to confront the question of "Why is this taking so long?" many, many times.

Here are some tips for fighting that natural, human response so you can err more on the side of a preschooler with self-control than our angry, impatient cartoon figure example.

IDENTIFYING IMPATIENCE

1. **Seek to recognize when it arises.** When you feel the draw to make a rash or impulsive decision, you're likely operating out of impatience. Catch yourself before you act.
2. **Think it through.** Hold off on making a conclusion or decision, and think first of what triggered the response. Then think out what other emotions arrive on the impatience train: perhaps anger, sadness, guilt, anxiety . . . Are any of those emotions helpful to your situation?
3. **Map out the potential outcome of the decision or action you were tempted to take as a result of these feelings.** Would it move you forward? Is it really the best action or decision?

CHANGING YOUR RESPONSE

Once you've become more aware of the moments where impatience sets in and have attuned your mind to map out the pitfalls of acting on that emotion and the others that tend to team up with it, you can leverage some of these strategies to move forward in a more productive way.

1. **Breathe.** I'm pretty sure we all grew up with parents who counted to ten and encouraged us to do the same, or even raised our children with Daniel the Tiger's "When You Feel So Mad" song, which instructs kids to take a deep breath and count to four. There is wisdom in both, as taking deep, slow breaths is proven to slow your heart rate and relax your body—which has a natural response to stress, anger, impatience, etc. If four deep breaths is all it takes, fantastic! But the general rule of thumb is ten. Sometimes you need twenty or thirty. Keep going until you can feel the emotions fade away. Becoming focused on your breath will also pull your mind away from the situation at hand, allowing you to come back to it more calmly and be more thoughtful in your response or action. Take the time to breathe for yourself and those around you, who can easily become collateral damage when you act or respond at the height of these emotions.

2. **Assess.** Before returning your thoughts to the situation that created the feeling of impatience, take note of your body's natural response and focus on relaxing all of those tense muscles. Our bodies and emotions operate off the same electrical wiring, so they are closely connected. Take the time to release that tension; it'll serve you and your decision-making well.

3. **Mindset.** Once your heart rate has slowed and your muscles have relaxed, switch to focusing on your mind. Can you now process the situation differently? Can you put on your good-seeker glasses and look at things from a more positive perspective? Keep trying until you can shift your mindset.

4. **Evaluate your needs.** As we were told as children and likely will tell our own, sometimes the stirring of these less-than-productive emotions stem from hunger (hangry much?), thirst, or the body crying out for another form of self-care. Identify what your physical body needs and take care of it before returning to the situation at hand.

If impatience, anger, and/or perfectionism are things you struggle with regularly, there is no harm in looking into Cognitive Behavioral Therapy. Think of it as just another tool to better understand how you as a perfectly imperfect and awesome individual work. Stress is ever-present on any success journey, so learning strategies for handling it more effectively can only help you to become more successful.

PRESSURE VERSUS PASSION

In another of my most recent reads, *Creating the Impossible: A Ninety-Day Program to Get Your Dreams Out of Your Head and into the World* by Michael Neill, the author breaks down the cause of our impatience in a wonderful way. He boils it down to pressure, the pressure we create around the deadlines we have or have given ourselves. There is so much truth in what he explains, which is that "There is no pressure preexistent in the world or inherently present in any given situation."[6] Think about that for a moment. The pressure we feel in any situation is created in our own minds, through our own thoughts. If we can control the pressure we feel, we will be less likely to turn to impatience in response.

Yes, it's important to stick to the goals and deadlines that we have established for chasing after our dreams. However, when we start to feel impatience stir, we need to stop and evaluate whether we are creating unproductive pressure that will lead to less-than-clear decision-making or lack of self-control. Motivation and passion should be the elements pushing us toward achievement, not pressure as it often brings with it the less productive emotions and reactions, such as impatience, anger, frustration, and desperation.

The fact that pressure is often present when we are staring at a deadline doesn't mean that the deadline is the cause of said pressure; it's simply a result of our own thoughts. How can you tell the difference between being pushed by pressure versus motivation or passion? My suggestion is to look in the mirror or simply stop and evaluate your physical response. What is your facial expression? How does your body feel? If you look stressed and tense, you're probably feeling pressure. If you're feeling strong, determined, and even have a happy or content expression on your face, you're likely feeling motivated and passionate. Take the time to adjust your thoughts, shifting to the passion and motivation you feel about completing the task at hand, tapping into those more positive drivers to move away from the impatience trap.

As we discussed in chapter 4, wiring yourself to achieve milestones that get you to your end goal requires battling both impatience and procrastination. For many of you, patience can feel like procrastination. *Don't both involve delay or not making progress?* you may be thinking. Nope. Patience is waiting for the seed you planted to grow and celebrating the task you've completed (planting the seed), whereas procrastination is avoiding planting the seed in the first place.

Over the course of my life, I've battled impatience far too many times to count. The techniques above have helped me tremendously, and I can attest to the value in acting on patience versus impatience. I can't think of a time where a decision I made out of impatience resulted in an ideal scenario. So embrace patience, celebrate how far you've come, and give those amazing success seeds the time they need to grow.

8

––––––▪===========▪––––––

KEEP ON KEEPING ON

"Success is not a matter of mastering subtle, sophisticated theory, but rather of embracing common sense with uncommon levels of discipline and persistence."

—Patrick Lencioni[1]

When I started college and made an agreement with my parents to contribute to the financial obligations of my education, I tried out a number of different jobs to cover my part. This included telesales with my older brother as my manager, selling roses out of a van, cashier at my local Grease Monkey, file clerk at a law firm, sales assistant at Targus, and eventually, my first recruitment tech-startup gig at GoJobs. One of the most important lessons I learned from all those jobs was the power of persistence and perseverance. Between my brother's sales coaching and the . . . unique . . . team environment I experienced packing boxes of roses from a warehouse into a van and "merching" all over town, I learned the Rule of Ten: it takes ten noes to get one yes. The mindset that was instilled in me was to not allow the noes to get you down; it just meant you were that much closer to a yes. I learned to trick myself into getting excited when I heard the word no and continue the countdown to my next yes.

This is the same mindset I have attempted to take with me in every endeavor, and I encourage you to adopt it as well. At the heart of that mindset is the spirit of persistence and perseverance. The Oxford dictionary defines persistence as, "Firm or obstinate continuance in a course of action in spite of difficulty or opposition," and, "Perseverance as persistence in doing something, despite difficulty or delay in achieving success."[2] The two go hand in hand and require patience to press on through delays, roadblocks, etc.

Let's face it, whatever we aim to achieve is going to come with many noes, delays, obstacles, difficulties, missteps, you name it. We can choose to feel defeated by them, or we can do the countdown, keep pressing on, and keep the faith that we can overcome whatever obstacles litter our path. The trick is in learning to use each no, obstacle, roadblock, or mistake as a tool to propel you toward your goal. Far better than letting those negative moments defeat you and end your quest right then and there.

FAILURE BREEDS GRIT

I've always been intrigued by success stories, and my experience working with startups made me wonder why more people don't choose the path of entrepreneurship. I have always been called a dreamer, and regardless of the spirit in which the label was placed on me, I've worn it like a badge of honor. In my view, entrepreneurs are dreamers with a mission. They are the ultimate goal-getters. I admire anyone with the passion and drive to chase after a dream, create something new or uniquely them, something with a purpose. When I created my consulting business and first started toying with the idea of wearing the entrepreneur label myself, I did what I always do: I began studying and researching anything I could get my hands on to better understand the new role I was taking on.

Given my admiration for this special breed of human, I was fairly shocked to learn that the vast majority of startups fail. According to the Small Business Administration in 2019, a whopping 90 percent fail, 21.5 percent in their first year.[3] That's a different perspective than what seems to be a continual stream of overnight successes, at least according to the news we outsiders see. Among the top reasons business owners attribute to this failure rate are funding (or running out of whatever funding was attained), being in the wrong market, bad partnerships, poor marketing, and lack of industry expertise. The No. 1 piece of advice Investopedia gives for future entrepreneurs to avoid failing is to *set goals*. Another of their top suggestions is *don't quit!* [4]

No matter what the nature of the achievement you seek is, tapping into the success mindset we've been discussing is critical to beating the odds. Being a student of whatever you aim to succeed at, having clearly defined goals, and persevering no matter how daunting the road seems are absolutely imperative. Here are some examples of perseverance to consider:

◊ *The Shack* by William P. Young was rejected by twenty-six publishing houses. The book has now sold more than 20 million copies and was made into a movie that grossed more than $57 million. [5]

◊ Michael Jordan, if you can believe it, didn't make the varsity basketball team his sophomore year. He didn't give up. He worked incredibly hard on the junior varsity team and went on to become one of the greatest basketball players of all time. [6]

◊ *Chicken Soup for the Soul* by Jack Canfield and Mark Victor Hansen was rejected by 130 different publishers. They've now sold more than 500 million copies. [7]

◊ Thomas Edison, the inventor of the light bulb, tried more than ten thousand times before he nailed it. Edison had this to say about the experience, "I have not failed. I've just found ten thousand ways that won't work." [8] Edison chose to leverage each failed attempt as a lesson in what wouldn't work, then went right back to his lab using what he'd learned until he found the magic formula.

◊ Jan Koum, founder of WhatsApp, grew up in Ukraine in a house with no running water and a school without an inside bathroom. When Koum and his mother immigrated to the United States, they had to live off of government assistance to get by. No doubt inspired by his mother's bravery in leaving Soviet-era Ukraine with her son, Koum began learning about computers in high school, and while he barely graduated, he was able to land a security tester job at Ernst and Young after high school. He worked his way up the ladder into leadership and eventually applied for a job at Facebook with his friend, Brian Acton. They were both rejected. With the extra time on their hands, they came up with the idea for WhatsApp.[9] Roughly five years after making that idea a reality, Facebook paid $21.8 billion to acquire the company.[10]

In each of these examples, can you imagine if they'd given up just before what would ultimately mean success for them? Think about babies who try and fall countless times before learning to crawl, walk, and talk. They don't give up. They just keep trying. Somewhere between the transition from childhood to adulthood, we mature and get more selective in the things we will put our energy into and are willing to fail at over and over again until we get it. That's not inherently bad, but we must not lose the power of persistence and perseverance in the things that matter most to us.

Any one of the stories above easily could have turned out differently if they hadn't tapped into that power, shirked off the fear of failure, and found ways to learn from those disappointing experiences where they were rejected or didn't get it right. That power lies inside us all. It simply takes a growth mindset and setting yourself up for success by managing your motivation, building discipline, and crafting micro-goals to ensure that you are constantly working toward your end goal. In the previous chapter, I referenced studies conducted by Angela Duckworth and her book *Grit*. In the book, Duckworth shares her definition of grit:

Perseverance + Passion = Grit

Again, in all of her findings, grit outweighs talent. You can have all the potential in the world, but if you don't do anything with that potential, what do you have to show for it? Nothing.

Similar to the ultimate conclusions of the Marshmallow Test, character traits such as self-control and grit can be learned. So don't throw your hands up in the air and think you need to give up if these are traits you feel you are lacking. Based on her findings, Duckworth argues that there are four key elements to tapping into the grit within: (1) interest, (2) practice, (3) purpose, and (4) hope.[11]

Let's take a deeper look at these elements and how you can maximize each of them to achieve the grit your goals require:

1. **Interest.** The first critical step to building your perseverance skills is identifying your passions. Let's face it, you're not going to tap into your grittiest self if you aren't charging toward a goal you are truly passionate about. If you're struggling to achieve the goal you've set, stop to consider just how passionate you are about it. Can you tie the goal to something you are very passionate about that is related or can come to fruition as a result of achieving your goal? Whatever it is, find a way to anchor your passion to your goal so you can more easily access the grit within.

2. **Practice.** If you've followed along the steps I've outlined in previous chapters, you should be making great progress on this element. To tap into perseverance, we must deliberately practice it by setting goals and challenging ourselves. It's important to set stretch goals, but remember that when you're starting from scratch, that could be a fifteen-minute task initially. Find a balance between what is believable and achievable and what will stretch your limits. Doing so in small increments (fifteen minutes) is absolutely helpful. Meet yourself where you're at and continue to push yourself in small doses; you will get there if you practice. It's like strength training. You wouldn't set a goal to bench press three-hundred pounds by going out on day one and putting three-hundred

pounds on the bar, would you? No. You work your way up to build the muscle as you go. The same goes for any character trait you are building.

3. **Purpose.** This is where chapter 2 and discovering your Why (or Whys) is critical. Unearthing the impact we seek to have on the world and those around us is key to tapping into passion. It is your purpose. If you are struggling with identifying your passion or connecting your purpose to the goal you are chasing, go back to chapter 2 and do the work to identify your Whys.

4. **Hope.** Plain and simple, the belief that your effort matters and will lead to the achievement of your goal and have a positive impact on your future is key to developing perseverance and grit. If you struggle to remain hopeful, catch yourself and go back to your Whys. Envision the "after," and remind yourself that effort is the only thing standing between you and your achievement.

On any success path, the only way to actually "fail" is to quit. Still stuck on the concept of failure? I'll remind you of Thomas Edison. Would you consider him a failure? He failed thousands of times before finally getting it right. A single failure doesn't mean the end, only quitting does. Once you've developed your grit muscles, you'll be an unstoppable goal-getting machine.

For over a decade now, I've struggled with hypothyroidism, which basically means my thyroid doesn't function optimally, leaving my metabolism much slower than it should be and making it that much more difficult to lose weight. Early on, I refused to believe the diagnosis and believed all my normal go-tos to lose those pesky pregnancy pounds would work—it worked for the Freshman 15 (*cough, cough,* twenty), so my thought was surely it would work now. Ha! Wrong. My focus on my children, husband, and career prevented me from realizing (for years, sadly) that I'd essentially given up on the idea that I could ever get out from under the weight I'd gained throughout my three pregnancies.

As my children grew, it was easier to remember to think about myself; I realized I'd still yet to shed the baby weight, even though my children were no longer babies. For years I tried diet after diet, only to learn that a diet wasn't the solution. I needed to change my lifestyle. This was another area in which I encountered impatience time and again, often leading to what I call the F-its, in which you give up and succumb to the fact that you just aren't getting anywhere—at least, not as quickly as you'd like. After much prayer, research, and about the third or fourth time I came across 75 Hard on social media, I decided it was a sign. The more I learned about the program, the more I realized it was exactly the lifestyle reset I needed. Little did I know how apparent it would make my back-then lack of grit, which was quickly, and thankfully, fortified as I started the program.

The process of completing 75 Hard taught me many things I've already shared with you: how to steel yourself to develop the habits you want to have, how to set micro-goals, and just how fulfilling and helpful it is to release those happy, little brain chemicals daily. In truth, 75 Hard changed my approach to everything, unlocking the grit that was always there but often sitting on a dusty shelf internally when it came to my personal health. That grit is the how and why I continue the lifestyle habits I developed during 75 Hard as well as how I completed one of the more daunting goals I've ever had—writing my first book.

All the dreams you once thought you could never achieve suddenly become possible when you tap into the success mindset. All that's required is an investment in keeping that mindset focused by Identifying Your Purpose, seeking to learn from all the obstacles that will find their way to you, keeping a positive outlook, and having an unshakeable faith. You got this!

9

LIFTING OTHERS UP

There is nothing quite like the fulfillment of watching someone you've mentored reach new heights. I've sometimes felt more pride in the successes of those I've helped than in my own achievements. After you have reached your goal (and that's *when*, not *if*), it's time to continue in your search for meaningful success by lifting up those around you.

Now, whether you've achieved your goal yet or not, let's think about the days, weeks, or months after that success. You'll likely be thinking, *I did it! What now?* If you're a true goal-getter, you might find it difficult to simply be where you are once you've achieved your big, hairy, audacious goal. For starters, please take the time to celebrate your incredible achievement! The most surefire way to enter a cycle of burnout is to *not* pause, acknowledge, and enjoy the fruits of your labor. Constantly jumping from one massive goal to the next can cause serious wear and tear on you mentally, physically, and spiritually. Besides, in pausing to celebrate and enjoy the success you've achieved, you will be able to optimize your next plan and path by giving all the above time to integrate and process the experience of your latest accomplishment.

If you can look around you after achieving your goal and seek ways to give back by helping others, you'll tap into a greater purpose and sense of fulfillment. If you lead a team of people, whether at work or just in life, you'll be so on fire about your accomplishment that the impact you can have to lift others up and help them achieve their goals will be that much greater. Your wins will bring *them* more inspiration and drive. No masks for this one, my friends—spread that inspiration and drive anywhere and everywhere you can! In my life and career, I've been blessed to have the opportunity to help others and have been blown away by the gratitude I've received by doing what I consider the simplest of things to help them.

Let's play with a little rock-climbing metaphor. Say that the last goal you achieved was one heck of a difficult climb and you're ready to do it again or find an even more difficult rock to climb. Along the way, you've learned a lot about strategies for climbing faster, about keeping yourself safe, what tools to use, etc. *After* pausing to celebrate the achievement, you arrive at your next challenge, and you see a newbie staring up at the climb ahead looking awfully hesitant, nervous, scared perhaps. You can either ignore this newbie and their cold feet, go about your climb, and look forward to posting it all on Instagram. Cool, cool. *Or* you could go over to the newbie and offer an encouraging word. Maybe even talk them through what gets you in the right mindset to climb and mention that you get nervous before every climb too and tell them that they've got this. Shoot, you could even offer to buddy up and coach them through the climb for as long as they need.

Picture all those scenarios and the feelings that would result from each. If you go the ignore-the-newbie path, you might feel guilty halfway up the climb because you remember a time when you were in their shoes. If you go the pep-talk route, you will likely feel good about helping someone out, but perhaps still wonder if they're going to be alright and whether you should have helped them more. Now, if you put on your coach hat and take the time, for however long, to guide them before or during the climb, you might get annoyed from time to time at the constant questions or the fact that your pace is now slower because you keep having to stop to help them out, but when you finish the climb together, you not only get to celebrate (and post it on IG, sure) *your* achievement, but also theirs too. And man, oh man is secondhand excitement intoxicating!

I'll let you in on a little secret: the achievement high from having a hand in someone else's success beats solo achievement by about a mile. Even more fulfilling is the gratitude you will generally receive in turn. Oh, and the icing on the cake is seeing that person pass it on. Think about that. Imagine the pay-it-forward ripple *you* have the power to create.

> *"The meaning of life is to find your gift. The purpose of life is to give it away."*
> —PABLO PICASSO[1]

> *"A spiritual gift is given to each of us so we can help each other."*
> —1 CORINTHIANS 12:7[2]

GREATER HAPPINESS AHEAD

Anyone who has worked with me knows my answer to, "What do you want to do next?" For many years, that answer has been, "I will go wherever I am needed and can have the greatest impact." To some, this may seem less than inspired or perhaps noncommittal. For me, it's representative of a prayer I've prayed since childhood: to be used as a vessel for good and to have reassurance that the path I'm on is leading me toward being a vessel, to let my light shine and light the way for others. My commitment to being flexible and going with my gut about the purpose behind whatever I am working on has led me to incredible growth and success.

Did you know that giving of your time, talents, and effort is actually good for your health? It's true. There are several studies showing that giving is not only good for the recipient, but also the giver, leading to greater happiness, satisfaction, a self-esteem boost, and even lower blood pressure potentially. You might be asking what this has to do with a book about the mindset for success, and I'm glad you asked.

If you've read the previous chapters, you understand that my goal is to provide tips and advice for how to achieve meaningful success. It can be confusing to reach one big achievement and wonder, *Okay, now what?* This is why I suggest looking around from the top of that amazing mountain you just climbed and see where you can lend a hand and bring others to the top of their mountain as well. Success can be lonely, but bringing others along is a tremendous feeling for all involved.

True success is sustained fulfillment. There is only so much meaning and fulfillment you can get out of achieving your own goals, and most often people find that giving back fuels greater fulfillment and generates even greater achievements for oneself. There are so many quotes about lifting others up, sharing your gifts, and lending a helping hand. Why? Because as the proverbial saying goes, "A rising tide lifts all boats." You can be the tide.

During my career, I've had so many wonderful opportunities to mentor and guide members of my teams, colleagues, friends, and family members. And it doesn't take a lot to get a mentorship relationship going. If you are in a leadership role, you are in the most ideal spot to make it happen. All you've got to do is invest the time to learn about your people. Whether you hired them all directly or not, take the time to learn about their background and inquire about their goals and what gives them fulfillment. Just asking those questions led me to finding an incredibly overqualified customer success rep on my team (I inherited the team, so I was on a mission to get to know every single one of them and truly understand the resources and talents I had on the team) who happened to have a skill another department was in need of. After discovering this, it didn't take more than a nudge to get him to shadow that department, land a new role, and subsequently increase revenue by $1 million by utilizing his knowledge and skill. The pride I felt in his achievement still makes me smile.

Another of my favorite stories is of a woman whose role I was revising during a reorganization, and she was beginning to feel a bit like she was going to befriend "Wilson" in short order (on her own island).[3] In each one-on-one meeting, we talked about the continuing evolution of the team, her role, and dove into her goals and interests. Initially, she swore up and down to me that she had zero interest in learning Microsoft Excel (I'm a data nerd, even in private life, so Excel and Google Sheets were always topics of conversation) and didn't see herself jumping into data and reporting. I do recall jokingly making a bet with her that, by the end of that year, she'd love it. My prediction was correct, and I even received an update from her recently that she'd taken it upon herself to learn SQL, a programming language for reporting on and analyzing data, and was now preparing to take on team reporting to ease the burden on the development team. Her excitement over mastering these skills that once seemed so foreign and out of her wheelhouse is something I share with her. What did it take for me to nudge her in that direction? Not much. She did the work; I simply asked the questions and opened the door by being a cheerleader and resource for her on her journey.

At times, the thought of being leaned on as a "mentor" can be intimidating, leaving you wondering if you are going to have the answers for them. What I've found time and time again is that the role of mentor (a.k.a. giving my time to help another) has challenged me and allowed me to grow in ways I never expected. In fact, it's what gave me the confidence to start my own consulting business. Had I not taken on the role of mentor and learned this lesson, who knows if or when I would have gone out on that limb.

GIVE WHAT YOU CAN

Looking back at my career, I am so grateful for the support system that I was blessed to have in my personal and professional life. Every time I struggled with confidence, I not only had my husband and family to remind me that I could do it, but also some of the best bosses and colleagues I could have ever asked for. One of the most impactful moments I recall is when my boss gifted his entire leadership team with a few powerful books. His name is Allan Jones, and at the time, he was the chief marketing officer at ZipRecruiter. Allan has since founded Bambee, has been named one of Goldman Sachs's one hundred most intriguing entrepreneurs of 2021, and has ranked as a *Forbes* Best Startup in America in 2020, 2021, and 2022.[4]

One of the books Allan gifted me was *Lean In: Women, Work, and the Will to Lead* by Sheryl Sandberg. I'll never forget after finally getting around to reading it, I barged into his office and slammed my hand on his desk saying, "Oh my God, it's *not* just me!"[5] The smile and look of knowing on his face was just what I needed to see. In addition to his stories of feeling the same way, the book opened my eyes to the imposter syndrome that was the cause of my inconsistent self-confidence. More than that, it created a fire in me to help other women and minorities understand that no, it's not just you, and we can overcome imposter syndrome by defeating the internal bias we often develop through our experiences of bias toward us.

That one thoughtful gift completely changed my course and passion. It opened my eyes to a new path and more fulfillment than I had ever imagined. I will always be grateful to Allan for not just the gift of a few amazing books but also for seeing what I needed to read and opening my eyes to a new purpose.

There are millions of people in the United States and around the world who are significantly less likely to go after that next promotion or possibly even be considered because of the conscious and unconscious bias that surrounds us all. While there are many movements today to open doors to those less likely to be given opportunities, we still have to face the inequalities and inequities that continue to exist for women, people of all different shades, and members of the LGBTQ+ community. The simple fact is those of us with advantage or who have managed to rise above bias and "broken the odds" have a human obligation to lend a helping hand to those with the odds stacked against them.

If you are a business-minded person, I can understand that last sentence feeling like a tall order. You are busy. You have a lot of responsibility. Unless you fundamentally disagree with the notion that we should do the human thing and help others who need more help, you're probably fighting internally on how much of your time is enough to make a difference and how much time you feel you can actually give to those efforts. For starters, let me clarify that help comes in so many different sizes and shapes. It can be as simple as providing encouragement, offering a tip, or it can look like full-blown mentorship. All that matters is that you give what you can give.

Let's clarify the difference between equality and equity for a moment. In one of my favorite courses in college, sociology, I recall diving into the concept of leveling the playing field. For years, we were taught that equality was the measure of treating everyone fairly and doing what was right by those who don't have the same opportunities as others. As you can see in the image below, equality and treating everyone the same doesn't give everyone the same opportunity for success. Sure, equality is great, but what's really needed is equity: giving everyone what they need, factoring in their differences and unique situations, in order to succeed. The simple fact is there are many in our world who aren't in a position to see the opportunities before them; they need a little extra assistance in order to see what could be, to understand what they could be, what they can achieve, and how to get there.

If you're still wondering what you can do to help those who are staring at the back of the fence versus seeing above it, look at the image below.

Figure 9.1. "Equality/Equity" by Angus Maguire demonstrates that equality is the equal giving of resources, while equity is giving resources to make everyone equal.

After performing a study in 2021, LeanIn found that, despite the fact that 57 percent of college graduates are women, they represent less than a quarter of C-suite positions—with women of color being only 4 percent of that disturbingly low representation. Men of color also represent a shockingly low 13 percent of C-suite position holders.[6]

How can you help? Give these underrepresented groups a *chance*. Look for opportunities to mentor women and people of color. Take the time to offer assistance.

As I described in some of my favorite mentorship success stories, mentorship and help really aren't all that complicated. You never know if asking a question, mentioning the potential you see in someone, or offering to be a sounding board and helping hand can light the fire that drives someone to incredible growth and achievement. Open the door to conversation, let them know you are there to help, and you will be amazed at how that simple act can affect their lives in a profound way.

> *TIP:* **Succeed through serving others. If you are inspired or fulfilled by something, do your best to bring that into your sphere of influence, offering it to those around you. There's something mystical— call it the law of attraction—that happens when you dole out good as often as possible: it seems to amplify in your sphere and come to you more and more frequently.**

In my own story, I can testify to the importance of those helping-hand moments and how they inspired and empowered me to continue evolving in my career. If it weren't for the many people who took a chance on a driven young woman who just wanted to grow and see how far I could go, I don't know that I ever would have gotten there or to this moment in time, writing a book to share with as many people as possible that what you dream of for your future *is* possible.

In keeping with my nature, I feel compelled to share a few examples of when I was the recipient of a helping hand. My entrance into the recruitment-technology industry was far smoother than what I'd expected of an industry change, thanks to Jonathan Duarte (CEO of GoJobs, at the time). Frankly, at that time, I'd yet to feel attached to any specific industry, as I was still figuring out where I fit and where I could find a good challenge as well as growth opportunities. The passion and knowledge Jon had for the industry was evident when we spent eight hours a day for my first couple of weeks diving into every layer of the industry—from customers to different types of partners, workflows, history, you name it. Whether he invested that time out of a need to get me up to speed or out of understanding my need to understand the whole picture, it was a time investment I hadn't expected but appreciated.

He listened to me each time I walked into his office and reported that I'd taken on something new and needed a new title . . . and a raise. The open communication I experienced under his leadership inspired confidence in me and certainly taught me a lot about how it felt to have a leader who didn't hesitate to invest time in me and help me to grow. My first experience of being recruited happened after being at his company for a little longer than a year and a half, at a point in which I felt I might need to stretch my wings a bit.

I felt a strong sense of loyalty given his personal investment in my rapid growth under him, and the fact that we were such a small company. I fully expected a guilt trip or some sort of negative reaction when I made up my mind to move on to a new challenge. None of that occurred. He didn't hold me back when I told him I needed to head off on a new path. He supported me, cheered me on, and just a few years ago he asked me to be part of his advisory board for his new company GoHire (I accepted). As I began advising him, he shared one of the most heartwarming sentiments I've ever received: during a coaching session with another employee, he mentioned my name, accomplishments, and that I was his biggest success story. He most certainly holds a place in my success story as well.

Another one of the most impactful helping-hand experiences I've had comes from the cofounders of ZipRecruiter: Ian Siegel, Ward Poulos, Joe Edmonds, and Will Redd. Ian approached me not long after I discovered how to hack my mindset to stop focusing on the frustrating and instead look for the blessing. It was an odd series of events that led to being recruited by him. We had both expressed concerns about the same partner's business model and had requested a meeting prior to an industry conference in Florida. Little did we know that the partner had decided to consolidate the meetings we requested into one. It wasn't until I ran into Ian in the hotel's Starbucks that we realized the car service they were sending to take us to their office was picking us both up and our meetings were at the same time.

During our ride, I was apparently wearing my heart on my sleeve when Ian asked me how work was going. He was someone I'd worked with for about a year as a partner, but I'm certain part of my unintended transparency was due to frustration and anxiety. After our meeting, I had a scheduled meeting with my current CEO about the fact that my compensation didn't match the role I was doing and was far from equitable to the person previously in the role, though they had a higher title than me. I was fully anticipating leaving that meeting disappointed. While I didn't disclose those details to Ian, he could tell I was frustrated and disappointed. His response? "If you're ever not happy there, I hope I'm your first phone call."

It didn't take long for me to make that phone call. In fact, it happened immediately after that meeting with my CEO, which wound up being even more disheartening than I'd anticipated. It's a strange experience to feel, on the one hand, so defeated that you begin to question whether you are simply out of touch with the reality of what you're worth and, on the other hand, feel so honored and encouraged by a respected CEO and cofounder that they want to be the first call you make when you're considering making a career move. Those conflicting emotions definitely did a number on me.

Though I was familiar with ZipRecruiter given they were a partner of the company I was still working for at the time, I decided to do my normal due diligence in preparation for my interview with the founders: is there more to the business than I'm aware of? Other products? Who are the founders? What are their backgrounds? Everything I learned made me giddy with excitement. This was a smart, legit startup with incredible potential and a team of founders who had resumes so impressive I felt a little like a fangirl when I first met them all face-to-face. What can I say? I'm more in awe of successful businesspeople who come from well-known and successful companies than celebrities.

True to myself, I walked into the interview with nerves I'm pretty sure nobody realized were there. I answered their questions competently, and when asked for how I'd plan to expand on the new product they were considering hiring me to work on, I had no issue telling them exactly how I thought they should run the business, what market segments were best to tackle first, how much revenue to expect from each segment, who the decision makers would be, and how closing deals would vary segment to segment, all based off of my experience and intuition. When I finished, I had a brief moment of worry, thinking perhaps I'd been too cocky. That was until Joe commented that he'd never had an interviewee walk in and tell him exactly how to run their business . . . and he loved it. Phew!

I received an offer immediately after my interview, which was incredibly exciting! These four successful, intelligent, and respectable cofounders saw me for my potential and gave me my first VP title. They valued my insights and gut. Over the four-and-a-half years I spent at Zip, I was given countless opportunities to grow and countless more to reassess my future goals. I've always been driven to challenge myself and see what I can accomplish, but the culture at Zip taught me that growth and success didn't just equate to a higher rung on the career totem pole.

Through their leadership, and the many, many inspiring and supportive colleagues I was blessed to work with there, I discovered my love of leadership. Early on, it dawned on me that my teenage dream of being a motivational speaker was happening. That was part of my job as a leader, and oh, how much I love that aspect of leadership! I quickly became addicted to giving to my employees and colleagues what I received from my leadership team and colleagues. The thrill of helping someone realize their value, their abilities, and, of course, their goals became more fulfilling to me than any fancy title ever could. Zip gave me one of the best work experiences of my life and changed me for the better—personally and professionally.

So you see, my success isn't my own. The handful of people listed above—and the many others I hold gratitude for in my heart that aren't mentioned by name—had a profound impact on my ability to see beyond the fence and succeed in ways I simply wouldn't have been able to see without their belief in me or their helping hands. They are the reason I feel so passionate about passing it on and the reason I encourage you to do the same.

Share your success mindset and faith with your family, friends, and team; you're sure to drive goals and passions that didn't exist before, encourage deeper purpose, and generate bigger and better goals in your own life.

CONCLUSION

BEGIN THE JOURNEY

There are so many different ways to classify success. This book will hopefully serve as a guide to adopting a success mindset in your life and inspiration for tapping into the greatest fulfillment possible: helping others to succeed as well. But first you must begin the journey for yourself.

If you've ever been on an airplane or had any sort of emergency training, you know that you have to first help yourself before you can help others. You can't help others if you are incapacitated in any way. And when it comes to any form of coaching, it's far more inspiring to come from a place of experience when pushing people to battle their fears, doubts, and worries. The "if I can do it, you can do it" message is more effective than "I've never tried, but I'm sure you can."

So do the work. Dive deep into the Whys behind any and every goal you're thinking about tackling, as surface-level ambitions are likely to be abandoned. Set yourself up for success by connecting your goals to deep-seated beliefs, values, and drives. Once you've mapped out the Whys, break down micro-goals to fortify your motivation, and build the little habits that will keep your progress consistent. Don't forget to take every ounce of learning from failures, because if you don't, you're missing out on tremendous growth opportunities.

Throughout the process, remember that you are the maker of your own destiny. You are the leader on this journey, and likely in other ways, across multiple aspects of your life. Refine your leadership style for your benefit and the benefit of others. And don't ever let fear cancel out your faith in yourself or the world around you. Fear may tell you otherwise, but if you didn't actually have faith that you could achieve your goals, you wouldn't even be toying with the idea of going for them.

Our journey here on Earth is one of constant and continual growth. Often, this growth comes in the aftermath of difficulties, trials, and tragedies. Getting through these situations builds character. If you can integrate all the learnings on your success path and share as many of them as possible with others, you will find more achievement and fulfillment than you ever dreamed possible. Keep your faith strong. Keep pressing on. Keep learning. And congrats on all your future successes!

ACKNOWLEDGMENTS

I am incredibly grateful to everyone that provided guidance on my journey and helped make *Faith Over Fear* a reality. I fully expected the process of finding a publisher to be one that would shake my confidence, but thanks to an industry colleague and friend Jess Miller-Merrell, I was referred to Brown Books Publishing Group. My first conversation with Milli Brown assured me that I'd found my publishing home. Working with the team at Brown Books has been nothing short of amazing. Milli's encouragement and knowledge eased my fears as a first-time author and built up my confidence and excitement for seeing this project through to the finish line.

My editors, Madelyn Schmidt Lindquist, Olivia Haase, and Sterling Zuelch provided wonderful feedback and suggestions throughout each phase of editing. They even managed to put a smile on my face several times with encouraging commentary on how much they loved various sections and phrases or even how they'd taken my advice. Their belief in this book and the message I feel so called to share made the editing process a joy. And for that, I'm truly appreciative.

I'd be remiss if I didn't mention a few more people who contributed to the person I am today, the lessons I've learned, and why I felt both the need and the confidence to write this book. Had Jonathan Duarte (CEO of GoHire) not taken a chance on an ambitious college student who applied to be his administrative assistant, but walked into his office suite ready to take over, who knows where I'd be now. Jon took the time to whiteboard (or brain dump, as we laughingly refer to it now) everything he knew about an industry that was entirely new to me. He listened to me each time I walked into his office and reported that I'd taken on something new and needed a new title. He didn't hold me back when I told him I needed to head off on a new path. He supported me, cheered me on, and we continue to collaborate to this day.

Shelly Marchegiani (former VP at TopUSAJobs.com) saw the inner saleswoman in me and took a chance on a sales newbie, launching my career in a whole series of new directions I wasn't anticipating. Don Firth (CEO of TopUSAJobs and a number of niche job boards) gave me countless opportunities to test and build skills in management, business development, partnerships, social media, etc. He also didn't hold me back when I announced I would be leaving for another new path.

Ian Siegel, Ward Poulos, Joe Edmonds, and Will Redd (ZipRecruiter cofounders) saw me for my potential and gave me my first VP title. They valued my insights and gut. They gave me one of the best work experiences of my life and cheered me on when I left to take on a new challenge. Their success and the hard work of everyone at ZipRecruiter that led to its IPO in 2021 allowed me to enter the stage of life I now enjoy, granting me time to focus on writing this book and seeing where that leads me.

Scott Hebert, Tim Dowd, and Dave Dickerson at Accurate Background showed me that I could succeed in an SVP role. Ethan Bloomfield (former CRO at TruckersReport.com and the person who taught me how to build a fun culture anywhere and everywhere in our ZipRecruiter days) brought the *Ethan and Mandy* show back to life at TruckersReport.com after bringing me my first real consulting gig.

Sam Elitzer (CEO of TruckersReport.com) welcomed my many, many ideas and pieces of advice throughout my time at TruckersReport.com and gave me an opportunity to flex my leadership consulting skills, which led to me seeing how I could branch out from consulting focused solely on client success or sales but to leadership in general. Sam's continuous reminders of the impact I've had on him as a leader as well as his leadership team fills my cup.

I am so grateful to the many friends and colleagues who have encouraged me on this journey. But most importantly, I thank my family. My husband, Brian Schaniel, handled the transition from retired wife to author wife without missing a beat. The moment I shared my idea for this book, he was all in. He ran interference with the kids whenever I needed "just a few more minutes" to write in quiet. He truly is my best friend, biggest supporter, and the best husband and father to our children. Our children's interest in this project took me by surprise. I love that they want to understand what I'm writing and are excited to tell their friends about it. It warms my heart that they've each requested a signed copy, and they will surely get it.

My husband, children, parents, and in-laws have been nothing short of amazing during this process and fully expect it to be a smashing success (no pressure). If this book touches just one soul, I will count it as a success. I do hope that, together, we can create a movement that inspires faith, big goals, and using fear as a tool instead of an anchor.

APPENDIX

MINDSET HACK

As mentioned in chapter 1, I highly recommend the Bible as a source of wisdom and a guide to find the good in any and every situation. I've found great comfort and motivation from several verses encompassing positive mindset, faith in the plan, and triumph in the midst of trial or failures. The mindset hack, the ability to turn a situation into good, I spoke of has improved my relationships and blessed me in big ways.

"We can rejoice, too, when we run into problems and trials, for we know that they help us develop endurance. And endurance develops strength of character, and character strengthens our confident hope of salvation."
—Romans 5:3-4 (NLT)[1]

*"Stop being angry! Turn from your rage!
Do not lose your temper — it only leads to harm."*
—Psalms 37:8 (NLT)[2]

"Dear brothers and sisters, when troubles of any kind come your way, consider it an opportunity for great joy. For you know that when your faith is tested, your endurance has a chance to grow."
—James 1:2-3 (NLT)[3]

"God blesses those who patiently endure testing and temptation. Afterward they will receive the crown of life that God has promised to those who love him."

—JAMES 1:12 (NLT)[4]

I've also recommended several books throughout these pages, all of which have taught me a lot and contributed to my success mindset. I've listed them here for you for ease of reference and hope they provide you with the same wisdom and enlightenment they've given me. (Please note, these books are listed in order of appearance in the book.)

Eric Jordan, *Emotional Intelligence Mastery: A Practical Guide to Improving Your EQ*[5]

Lee Cockerell, *Creating Magic: Ten Common Sense Leadership Strategies from a Life at Disney*[6]

Andy Frisella, *75 Hard: A Tactical Guide to Winning the War with Yourself*[7]

James Nestor, *Breath: The New Science of a Lost Art*[8]

Carol Dweck, PhD, *Mindset: The New Psychology of Success*[9]

Dr. Richard Wiseman, *The Luck Factor: Four Simple Principles that Will Change Your Luck—and Your Life*[10]

Ryan Holiday, *The Obstacle Is the Way: The Timeless Art of Turning Trials into Triumph*[11]

Piers Steel, *The Procrastination Equation: How to Stop Putting Things Off and Start Getting Stuff Done*[12]

Angela Duckworth, *Grit: The Power of Passion and Perseverance*[13]

Michael Neill, *Creating the Impossible: A Ninety-Day Program to Get Your Dreams Out of Your Head and into the World*[14]

Sheryl Sandberg, *Lean In: Women, Work, and the Will to Lead*[15]

NOTES

INTRODUCTION

1. Tony Woodall, "Action Is a Great Restorer and Builder of Confidence," *Goal Getting Podcast*, goalgettingpodcast.com, October 19, 2016. http://www.goalgettingpodcast.com/s2-e50-action-builds-confidence-norman-vincent-peale/.

CHAPTER 1

1. Marsha Petrie Sue, "Marsha Petrie Sue Bio 2021," Biography, Marsha Petrie Sue (website), last updated 2021. https://www.marshapetriesue.com/about.

2. Eric Jordan, *Emotional Intelligence Mastery: A Practical Guide to Improving Your EQ,* (Pine Peak Publishing, 2016).

3. John Nemo, "You've Never Heard of Edwin Barnes, but He Has Your Blueprint to Success," *The Business Journals*, September 24, 2014. https://www.bizjournals.com/bizjournals/how-to/growth-strategies/2014/09/youve-never-heard-of-edwin-barnes-but-he-has-your.html.

4. Joe Holley, "Obituaries of George Dantzig," *Washington Post*, May 19, 2005. https://supernet.isenberg.umass.edu/photos/gdobit.html.

5. Jer. 29:11 (New International Version).

6. Lee Cockerell, *Creating Magic: Ten Common Sense Leadership Strategies from a Life at Disney* (New York: The Doubleday Publishing Group, 2008).

CHAPTER 2

1. Andy Frisella, "75 Hard," 44Seven Media, last updated 2022. https://andyfrisella.com/pages/75hard-info.

2. Andy Frisella, *75 Hard: A Tactical Guide to Winning the War with Yourself* (44Seven Media, 2020).

3. Tainya C. Clarke, PhD, MPH; Patricia M. Barnes; Lindsey I. Black; et al. "Use of Yoga, Meditation, and Chiropractors Among U.S. Adults Aged 18 and Older," *NCHS Data Brief*, no. 325, National Center for Health Statistics (November, 2018). https://www.cdc.gov/nchs/products/databriefs/db325.htm?mod=article_inline.

4. Lachlan Brown, "25 Surprising Meditation Statistics Everyone Needs to Know," HackSpirit, last updated February 10, 2021. https://hackspirit.com/25-surprising-meditation-statistics-everyone-needs-to-know/.

5. Phil. 4:8 (New Living Translation).

6. "Long Term Benefits of Meditation Revealed," *The Daily Meditation*, accessed July 1, 2021. https://www.thedailymeditation.com/ways-to-use-meditation.

7. Juliana Spicoluk, Mark Spicoluk, "The 14 Day Meditation Journey—Impact Your Life with a Beautiful New Habit!" YouTube.com playlist, *Boho Beautiful Yoga*, last updated February 20, 2022. https://www.youtube.com/playlist?list=PLb09q0R-7gAwS5dzSXP5sryVkKMuySB7LM.

8. James Nestor, *Breath: The New Science of a Lost Art* (New York: Riverhead Books, 2020).

CHAPTER 3

1. Rm. 5:3-4 (NLT)

2. Carol Dweck, PhD, *Mindset: The New Psychology of Success* (New York: Penguin Random House, 2006).

3. Alan S. Cowen and Dacher Keltner, "Self-report Captures 27 Distinct Categories of Emotion Bridged by Continuous Gradients," *Proceedings of the National Academy of Sciences*, vol. 114, no. 38 (September 5, 2017). https://doi.org/10.1073/pnas.1702247114.

4. Ward Andrews, "Love vs. Fear," Design.org, October 2, 2019, https://design.org/love-vs-fear/.

5. Matt Weinberger, "This Is Why Steve Jobs Got Fired from Apple—and How He Came Back to Save the Company," *Insider*, July 31, 2017. https://www.businessinsider.com/steve-jobs-apple-fired-returned-2017-7.

6. Steve Jobs, "Steve Jobs's 2005 Stanford Commencement Address," June 12, 2005, Standford University, Stanford, California, video, 15:04. https://news.stanford.edu/2005/06/12/youve-got-find-love-jobs-says/.

7. Ben Mattison, "Women Aren't Promoted Because Managers Underestimate Their Potential," *Yale Insights*, September 17, 2021. https://insights.som.yale.edu/insights/women-arent-promoted-because-managers-underestimate-their-potential.

8. Oprah Winfrey, "Oprah Winfrey Commencement Speech | Harvard Commencement 2013," May 30, 2013, Tercentary Theatre at Harvard University, Cambridge, Massachusetts, video, 28:59. https://news.harvard.edu/gazette/story/2013/05/oprah-winfrey-commencement-speech-harvard-commencement-2013/.

9. Richard Wiseman, *The Luck Factor: Four Simple Principles that Will Change Your Luck—and Your Life* (United Kingdom: Arrow, 2004).

10. Richard Yates, *Revolutionary Road* (New York: Vintage Books, 1961).

11. Paulo Coelho, *The Alchemist* (New York, New York: HarperCollins, 1998).

12. Ryan Holiday, *The Obstacle Is the Way: The Timeless Art of Turning Trials into Triumph* (New York: Portfolio/Penguin, 2014).

13. Joyce Meyer, *Trusting God Day by Day: 365 Daily Devotions* (New York: Hodder & Stoughton, 2012).

CHAPTER 4

1. Thai Nguyen, "4 Ways to Hack Your Brain Chemicals to Become More Productive," *Entrepreneur*, July 27, 2016. https://www.entrepreneur.com/article/279717.

2. Larry Shaffer, "You Really Can Learn as Much from Failure as You Do Success," Fast Company & Inc. (website), June 19, 2022, https://www.fastcompany.com/90761446/you-really-can-learn-as-much-from-failure-as-you-do-success.

3. Mark Divine, "SEALFIT—4 Tactics for Success," *Navy SEALS*, January, 2014. https://navyseals.com/3837/sealfit-4-tactics-success/.

4. Piers Steel, *The Procrastination Equation: How to Stop Putting Things Off and Start Getting Stuff Done* (New York: HarperCollins e-books, 2010).

CHAPTER 5

1. Oprah Winfrey, "Oprah Winfrey, Academy Class of 1989, Full Interview," Academy of Achievement, last updated September 29, 2022. https://achievement.org/achiever/oprah-winfrey/#interview.

2. "2020 Global Employee Experience Trends," Qualtrics, 2020 (electronically published), accessed January 11, 2021. https://www.qualtrics.com/research-center/employee-experience-trends/.

CHAPTER 6

1. Hamed Dehghanan, Fatemeh Gheitarani, Saeed Rahimi, and Khaled Nawaser, "A Systematic Review of Leadership Styles in Organizations: Introducing the Concept of a Task-Relationship–Change Leadership Network," *International Journal of Innovation and Technology Management*, vol. 18, no. 07 (October 19, 2021). https://doi.org/10.1142/S021987702130007X.

2. Paul Harris, "Elon Musk: 'I'm planning to retire to Mars'," *The Observer*, July 31, 2010. https://www.theguardian.com/technology/2010/aug/01/elon-musk-spacex-rocket-mars.

3. "20 Ways to Become a Better Leader," *CEO Magazine* (website), March 31, 2022. https://www.theceomagazine.com/business/management-leadership/leadership-quotes/.

4. Matthew Tempest, "Rice says 'thousands' of mistakes made in Iraq," *The Guardian*, March 31, 2006. https://www.theguardian.com/politics/2006/mar/31/foreignpolicy.uk.

5. Dave Feschuk, "Feschuk: Winning Wasn't the Only Thing for Coaching Icon Vince Lombardi," thestar.com, *Toronto Star*, December 18, 2010. https://www.thestar.com/sports/football/2010/12/18/feschuk_winning_wasnt_the_only_thing_for_coaching_icon_vince_lombardi.html.

6. A. H. Maslow, "A theory of human motivation," *Psychological Review*, vol. 50, no. 4, 370–396 (1943). https://doi.org/10.1037/h0054346

7. Femina. "Cover Story: Indra Nooyi Turned Around Pepsico with Strategic Redirection," Femina, August 2, 2021. https://www.femina.in/trending/achievers/indra-nooyi-turned-around-pepsico-with-strategic-redirection-200175.html.

8. Jim Mateja, Rick Popely, et al. "Imagine that," *Chicago Tribune*, February 10, 2006. https://www.chicagotribune.com/news/ct-xpm-2006-02-10-0602100378-story.html.

9. Joe McCarthy, "11 Quotes That Show Angela Merkel Is a True *Global Citizen*," *Global Citizen*, July 27, 2017. https://www.globalcitizen.org/en/content/11-quotes-that-show-angela-merkel-is-a-true-global/.

10. Nelson Mandela, *Long Walk to Freedom: The Autobiography of Nelson Mandela* (New York: Little, Brown and Company, 1995).

11. Ellen Johnson Sirleaf, "Ellen Johnson Sirleaf at Harvard Commencement," May 26, 2011, Tercentary Theatre at Harvard University, Cambridge, Massachusetts, video, 34:18. https://www.harvardmagazine.com/2011/05/ellen-johnson-sirleaf-commencement-speech.

12. *O, The Oprah Magazine*, vol. 4, no. 12, December 2003.

13. Jer. 29:11 (NIV)

CHAPTER 7

1. Walter Mischel, *The Marshmallow Test: Mastering Self-Control* (New York: Little, Brown and Company, 2014).

2. Angela L. Duckworth and Martin E.P. Seligman, "The Science and Practice of Self-Control," *Perspectives on Psychological Science*, vol. 12, no. 5 (September 1, 2017): 715-718. https://doi.org/10.1177/1745691617690880.

3. Angela Duckworth, *Grit: The Power of Passion and Perseverance* (New York: Scribner, 2016).

4. Jonny Miller, "Will Smith's Philosophy," Medium.com, March 24, 2013. https://medium.com/@jonnym1ller/will-smiths-philosophy-668f37dd51b1.

5. Lisa Respers France, "Will Smith addresses Oscars slap in new video," *CNN*, July 30, 2022. https://www.cnn.com/2022/07/29/entertainment/will-smith-chris-rock-oscars-slap/index.html.

6. Michael Neill, *Creating the Impossible: A Ninety-Day Program to Get Your Dreams Out of Your Head and into the World* (London: Hay House UK Ltd., 2018).

CHAPTER 8

1. Patrick Lencioni, *The Five Dysfunctions of a Team: A Leadership Fable* (San Francisco: Jossey-Bass, 2002).

2. "Persistence," Oxford Languages, accessed on August 25, 2022. https://www.google.com/search?q=persistence+meaning.

3. Suprotik Sinha, "How Many Startups Fail and Why?" Unboxing Startups, August 31, 2021. https://unboxingstartups.com/how-many-startups-fail-and-why/.

4. Sean Bryant, "How Many Startups Fail and Why?" Investopedia, last updated November 26, 2022. https://www.investopedia.com/articles/personal-finance/040915/how-many-startups-fail-and-why.asp.

5. William P. Young, *The Shack: Where Tragedy Confronts Eternity* (Los Angeles: Windblown Media, 2007).

6. Tim Ott, "Michael Jordan: 7 Facts About the Basketball Legend," Biography, October 28, 2021. https://www.biography.com/news/michael-jordan-facts#.

7. Chicken Soup for the Soul LLC, "Facts & Figures," Chicken Soup (website), accessed August 25, 2022. https://www.chickensoup.com/about/facts-and-figures.

8. Mary Bellis, "Famous Thomas Edison Quotes," ThoughtCo., last updated July 3, 2019. https://www.thoughtco.com/edison-quotes-1991614.

9. Hannah L. Miller, "Jan Koum: The Inspirational Story of the Founder of WhatsApp," Leaders (website), last updated February 28, 2022. https://leaders.com/articles/leaders-stories/jan-koum/.

10. Alison L. Deutsch, "WhatsApp: The Best Meta Purchase Ever?" Investopedia, last updated March 29, 2022. https://www.investopedia.com/articles/investing/032515/whatsapp-best-facebook-purchase-ever.asp.

11. Marguerite Ward, "4 things the grittiest people have in common, according to a psychologist." CNBC, last updated August 2, 2016. https://www.cnbc.com/2016/08/01/4-things-the-grittiest-people-have-in-common-according-to-a-psychologist.html.

CHAPTER 9

1. Good News Network, "'The Meaning of Life Is to Find Your Gift. The Purpose of Life Is to Give It Away.' – Pablo Picasso (Born 140 Years Ago)," Good News Network (website), October 25, 2021. https://www.goodnewsnetwork.org/picasso-quote-about-meaning-and-purpose/.

2. 1 Cor. 12:7 (NLT)

3. Robert Zemeckis, dir. *Cast Away*. 2000; 20th Century Fox DreamWorks Pictures.

4. Scott MacDonell, "Bambee Celebrated by Goldman Sachs for Entrepreneurship: Allan Jones, Founder & CEO of Bambee, Among 100 Most Intriguing Entrepreneurs at 2021 Builders + Innovators Summit," *Business Wire*, October 13, 2021. https://www.businesswire.com/news/home/20211013005339/en/.

5. Sheryl Sandberg, *Lean In: Women, Work, and the Will to Lead* (New York: Alfred A. Knopf, 2013).

6. Lauren Shufran, "Attracting Female Talent for a More Gender-Equitable Pipeline," Gem (website), November 11, 2021. https://www.gem.com/blog/attracting-female-talent.

APPENDIX

1. Rm. 5:3–4 (NLT)

2. Ps. 37:8 (NLT)

3. Jas. 1:2–3 (NLT)

4. Jas. 1:12 (NLT)

5. Eric Jordan, *Emotional Intelligence Mastery: A Practical Guide to Improving Your EQ* (Pine Peak Publishing, 2016).

6. Lee Cockerell, *Creating Magic: Ten Common Sense Leadership Strategies from a Life at Disney* (New York: The Doubleday Publishing Group, 2008).

7. Andy Frisella, *75 Hard: A Tactical Guide to Winning the War with Yourself* (44Seven Media, 2020).

8. James Nestor, *Breath: The New Science of a Lost Art* (New York: Riverhead Books, 2020).

9. Carol Dweck, PhD, *Mindset: The New Psychology of Success* (New York: Penguin Random House, 2006).

10. Richard Wiseman, *The Luck Factor: Four Simple Principles that Will Change Your Luck—and Your Life* (United Kingdom: Arrow, 2004).

11. Ryan Holiday, *The Obstacle Is the Way: The Timeless Art of Turning Trials into Tragedy* (New York: Portfolio/Penguin, 2014).

12. Piers Steel, *The Procrastination Equation: How to Stop Putting Things Off and Start Getting Stuff Done* (New York: HarperCollins e-books, 2010).

13. Angela Duckworth, *Grit: The Power of Passion and Perseverance* (New York, New York: Scribner, 2016).

14. Michael Neill, *Creating the Impossible: A Ninety-Day Program to Get Your Dreams Out of Your Head and into the World* (London: Hay House UK Ltd., 2018).

15. Sheryl Sandberg, *Lean In: Women, Work, and the Will to Lead* (New York: Alfred A. Knopf, 2013).

ILLUSTRATION CREDITS

CHAPTER 7

Figure 7.1. *Source:* https://coffeewiththelord.com/2015/10/02/im-patience-and-anger-two-wild-horses-that-need-to-learn-to-take-a-bridle/.

CHAPTER 9

Figure 9.1. *Source*: Image credit is given to Interaction Institute for Social Change (interactioninstitute.org) with art by Angus Maguire (madewithangus.com), "2-panel Equality/Equity illustration" (digital image), Center For Story-Based Strategy (website), (January 13, 2016). https://www.storybasedstrategy.org/permission-to-reproduce. Licensed under CC BY-NC 4.0 https://creativecommons.org/licenses/by-nc/4.0/.

ABOUT THE AUTHOR

Mandy Schaniel is the founder and CEO of Schaniel Consulting Inc., providing leadership and business coaching to start-ups looking to build a culture of inclusivity, progress, and success for both their business and employees. Her rise to leadership came early when she was recruited to join the executive team at ZipRecruiter as employee number nineteen. During her four-and-a-half years at ZipRecruiter, she helped lead the company to its first million-dollar month, built the company's first account management team, created a safe space for women and men to seek mentorship from growth-minded leaders like herself, and helped many on her team to reach the next step. The experience of being a foundational contributor to the success of ZipRecruiter led her to new opportunities. She took the lessons about culture and leadership she learned as VP of key account management and support at ZipRecruiter to her roles as SVP of client success at Accurate Background and EVP of client success at TruckersReport. com. She still applies those learnings and all that she's learned in between to her advisory roles at Intry and GoHire, and to anyone that seeks her mentorship. A truly growth-minded leader with an entrepreneurial spirit, Mandy seeks to keep spreading the knowledge she's gained with anyone looking to take the next step in their life. Mandy earned her BA in communications with an emphasis on print journalism from California State University, Fullerton, and earned her spot on the dean's list multiple times. Mandy lives in Southern California with her husband and three children.

Mandy Schaniel will be donating 10 percent of all revenues from this book to various charities and institutions that seek to provide cures, a helping hand, and support for those in need.